Demanding Peace

Demanding Peace

Christian Responses to War and Violence

A.E. Harvey

In collaboration with members of
The Council on Christian Approaches to Defence
and Disarmament
and The Churches Peace Forum

With an Appendix by
Brian Wicker

SCM PRESS

0 334 02789 6

Unless otherwise stated, biblical quotations are from
The Revised English Bible 1989

First published 1999
by SCM Press
9–17 St Albans Place, London N1 0NX

SCM Press is a division of
SCM–Canterbury Press Ltd

Typeset by Rowland Phototypesetting Ltd
Bury St Edmunds, Suffolk
Printed in Great Britain by Biddles Ltd
Guildford and King's Lynn

Contents

The following attended at least one of the meetings at which these issues were discussed:

Sir Hugh Beach
Myriel Davies
Gerald Drewett
The Rt Revd Tony Dumper
Sir Arthur Hockaday
Dr Bernard Hoose
The Revd Dr Anthony Harvey
Dr Peter Jarman
Prof. Norman Kember
Dr Tony Kempster
The Revd Dr Paul Oestreicher
The Revd Alan Race
The Revd Edwin Robertson
Dr Gwenda Thompson
Dr Non Vaughan-Thomas
The Revd Rachel Wadey
Brian Wicker
Dr Roger Williamson
The Revd Dr Kenneth Wilson

Preface

Shortly before he died in 1995, Sydney Bailey, the distinguished Quaker historian and mediator, suggested to a meeting of the Council on Christian Approaches to Defence and
Disarmament (of which he was a founder member) that the
pacifist stance to which he had been committed for the whole
of his life required fresh study and interpretation in view
of modern conditions of war-making and peace-keeping.
Meanwhile the World Council of Churches had launched
its *Programme to Overcome Violence* which the Churches'
Peace Forum (of the Council of Churches for Britain and
Ireland) was charged to disseminate. This too required theological analysis and reflection. The convergence of these two
interests resulted in the formation of a working party drawn
from the two bodies, which met over a period of two years
for a discussion of questions of war, violence and peace as
they appear at the end of the twentieth century.

Given the wide range of views represented (from those of
professional servicemen on the one hand to those of committed pacifists on the other) it was not to be expected that
every member would be able to endorse every sentence of
the book which resulted from these meetings. But they have
all generously agreed that I have compiled a fair account of
the opinions which were expressed, and I am grateful to
them for allowing me to incorporate both their verbal and
their written contributions into the main text without

specific acknowledgment. This book is the fruit of discussions that were both frank and sensitive between those who hold traditionally opposed views. But the greater part of the text, with all its shortcomings, is entirely my own.

We must also express our gratitude to Kenneth Wilson whose Research Institute at Queen's College Birmingham provided essential support for the expensive business of circulating successive drafts of the book to all members of the group.

The book was completed while NATO was launching air attacks on Serbian forces in the Balkans. In the view of many, using force and refraining from using force seemed equally likely to be fraught with horrendous consequences. Contemporary history could have provided no better, and no more tragic, illustration of the complexity of the issues which now challenge the Christian conscience in matters of war, violence and peace. We hope this book may make some small contribution to Christian thinking on these agonizing problems.

Anthony Harvey

Prologue: 'Not as the world gives . . .'

Peace I leave with you; my peace I give to you; not as the world gives do I give to you (John 14.27).

Our difficulty with this phrase is that in our Western culture there is no convention of 'giving peace'. Our greetings and farewells are hellos and goodbyes; they make no mention of peace. We wish our friends good luck, a safe journey, a quick recovery; but in English it sounds odd to wish them peace. Hence the artificiality of the little ceremony which most Christians are now encouraged to perform in church – 'Let us give one another the sign of peace.' We exchange a handshake or an embrace. But in the language of our culture this would normally mean something like 'How do you do?', 'I am glad to see you again.' The word that does *not* seem appropriate is 'peace'.

The same was true of the Greeks and Romans. 'Hail' and 'Farewell' are the nearest English equivalents to the greetings they normally exchanged with each other. To them, as to us, 'peace' would have sounded strange in this context. They would have been as puzzled as we are by the notion of the 'world giving peace'. But the Jews, like most semitic peoples, had a different convention. In greetings and farewells they said, as they still say, *shalom*, 'peace'. And this for good reason. Peace, in their culture, was regarded as the highest of earthly goods. To live at peace with foreign nations, at peace with other groups and communities, at peace with your friends and neighbours – this was one of God's greatest gifts, the most creative and desirable condition of society, something worth having at almost any cost – even, at times, at the price of a slight compromise with strict truth or honesty. Peace was what God willed for his people and included in his blessing: 'May the Lord look kindly upon you and give you peace' (Num. 6.26). And peace was what Jewish people instinctively wished for one another when they met: 'Peace be to you and peace be to your house, and peace be to all that you have' (I Sam. 25.6 NRSV).[1]

So, in the culture within which Jesus lived, to 'give peace' was as natural as it is unnatural in ours. There would have been nothing strange in talking of the world 'giving peace'. If you lived in that world, you would hear people 'giving peace' every day. But we must not imagine that it was a random or thoughtless greeting. It was appropriate only under certain circumstances. To give peace, you must have the right social position and sufficient credit. The circumstances must be appropriate. You must know the rules and observe the conventions.

Let us take a few examples. Jehu arrives with an armed force outside the town of Jezreel. Messengers go to meet him with the words, 'The king asks, "Is it peace?"' 'Peace?', said Jehu, 'What is that to do with you?' (II Kings 9.18); and later, when he meets King Joram, he justifies his refusal to 'give peace': 'Do you call it peace while your mother Jezebel keeps up her obscene idol-worship and monstrous sorceries?' (9.22). Force of arms gives a man the power to give or withhold peace. If he gives it, the gift is no idle greeting. It is the removal of a threat.

The same is true of anyone who has power over others. Take a king and his subjects. He has absolute power over them. If he gives them 'peace', they are safe; if he withholds it, they are at risk. David is in trouble with King Saul. He sends a message to the king by the king's son Jonathan, but is uncertain of the outcome. He confides to Jonathan: 'If he (Saul) says "Good", it will be peace[2] for your servant' (I Sam. 20.7). Again, the king's position enables him to give or withhold peace. If he gives it, it is more than a mere greeting. It is the removal of a threat which the king has the power to carry out.

It follows that even casual and everyday greetings were subject to certain conditions. The superior in society could 'give peace' to his inferior, and this would imply the absence of any threat. Peace was a kind of gift the rich could bestow on the poor, the strong on the weak: it was an assurance that though the master was in a position to make life difficult for his servant, the landlord for his tenant, the creditor for his debtor, he would not do so. As a greeting, therefore, giving peace implied social status. A beggar could not normally give peace to a rich man: he had no credit out of which to give it, no power to enforce a threat or to give an assurance of security. I say 'normally', because he might of course waylay him in a deserted place and threaten his social superior with brute force. In that case, his giving of peace would be meaningful and appropriate (though probably conditional on the promise of some reward). But in a crowded street, a greeting of 'peace' from a social inferior would be received as something of an insult. And there was always the possibility of a dangerous deception. 'Peace' could be given sneeringly or fawningly, the smile might not be genuine: 'Take me not off with the wicked . . . who give peace to their neighbour, while mischief is in their hearts' (Ps. 28.3 RSV).

We are beginning to see that the way the world 'gives peace' is more subtle and complicated than first appeared. But there is more. A man's resources for giving peace are not unlimited, any more than his credit is. He can give assurances of security and good intentions only to a limited number of people, those who are in some way dependent on him (his debtors, his tenants, his relatives). He cannot take on responsibility for the 'peace' of all and sundry – that would be to exaggerate his own importance and influence. The peace one can give, therefore, is like a commodity. It is not inexhaustible; it can be used up, so it must not be squandered. Gehazi is sent by Elisha to the dead son of the Shunammite woman. All Elisha's power and influence is concentrated upon the single task of reviving this boy. It must not be dissipated in casual encounters along the road. 'If you meet anyone on the way, do not stop to greet him; and if anyone greets you, do not answer' (II Kings 4.29). In much the same way Jesus' followers are told to 'exchange no greetings on the road' (Luke 10.4), not out of incivility or excessive haste, but because the 'peace' which their greeting would carry is a precious commodity, to be given only to those worthy of it:

> When you go into a house, let your first words be, 'Peace to this house.' If there is a man of peace there, your peace will rest on him; if not, it will return to you (Luke 10.5–6).

The commodity of peace is such that it can even be retrieved if it is distributed in the wrong place!

This last example brings us to a further point: some people *cannot* receive peace when it is offered to them. Who are these people? Some verses in Isaiah make this perfectly plain.

> Peace, peace, for all both far and near; I shall heal them, says the Lord. But the wicked are like a storm-tossed sea, a sea that cannot be still, whose waters cast up mud and dirt. There is no peace for the wicked, says my God (Isa. 57.19–21).

There is no peace for the wicked; therefore an element of moral judgment creeps even into an everyday greeting. I can give peace only to someone who is honest. If my tenant is about to cheat me, it will make no difference if I have assured him of his security by 'giving him peace'. He was not worthy to receive it, and I shall take him to court. The commodity of peace can have currency only in a society of the just and the good. If I give you peace I am making an assumption about your moral character. If I am wrong, my own power and influence will be diminished by your dishonesty and I shall have less credit out of which to give peace to others – unless I can retrieve my peace from you in time to prevent you from abusing it.

We now have some idea of 'peace as the world gives'. It is a greeting but more than a greeting. It is a genuine wish for the welfare of another. But to pronounce the wish is to claim some ability to promote that welfare. It implies that one has the appropriate social status for doing so, and it implies also a promise which it would be unrealistic to make to all and sundry. The peace one can confer is a limited commodity; moreover not all can receive it. Its proper distribution involves discriminating between the righteous and the wicked. Giving peace is not just a social, it is a moral activity.

It is against this background that we must now try to form a clearer picture of the peace which Jesus gives and which is *not* 'as the world gives'. But first, there is another activity to be considered: not peace-giving, but peace-making. Here our text is one of Jesus' Beatitudes:

> Blessed are the peacemakers; they shall be called God's children (Matt. 5.9).

This is not in itself a disturbing statement. We think of those who intervene in a quarrel and get the parties to agree; we think of those who are willing to mediate in angry disputes; we think of Count Bernadotte or Gunnar Jarring devoting themselves untiringly and heroically to securing peace in Jerusalem. It is not difficult to see why Jesus should have called such people 'blessed'. But is this what he meant?

We need to take note of the fact that this is unlikely to be a general comment of approval for people whom we already respect. It stands in the sequence of Jesus' Beatitudes, and these have the character of a challenge, not a pat on the back. The opening of the Sermon on the Mount proclaims nothing less than a reversal of normally accepted values and priorities. Blessed are the poor, the sorrowful, the meek – this is the exact opposite of our usual criteria for blessedness. Social approbation normally goes to the powerful, the distinguished, the wealthy; but Jesus apparently reverses the calculus. The point is pressed home in Luke's account, where the 'blessings' are followed by explicit 'woes':

'But alas for you who are rich . . . who are well fed now . . . who laugh now . . . when all speak well of you . . .' (Luke 6.24–6).

Evidently the point of the Beatitudes is that those who are really blessed are not those whom we would normally have expected to be so. In which case we must beware of assuming that when Jesus said 'Blessed are the peacemakers' he was saying exactly what most of us would say ourselves. Is there another explanation?

Let us take a cue from the other Beatitudes and ask: in the matter of strife, argument and dispute what are the qualities which would normally be admired? Those, presumably, which enable people to stand by their rights, to strengthen their arguments, to win their case, to obtain what they deserve. But what was Jesus' view? It is sometimes argued that the remainder of Matthew chapter 5 is intended to be a kind of commentary[3] on the Beatitudes, and that verses 21–26 are therefore a series of illustrations of 'Blessed are the peacemakers'. Whether or not this is correct, these verses are certainly relevant to our question. They run as follows:

You have heard that our forefathers were told, 'Do not commit murder; anyone who commits murder must be brought to justice.' But what I tell you is this: Anyone who nurses anger against his brother must be brought to justice. Whoever calls his brother 'good for nothing' deserves the sentence of the court; whoever calls him 'fool' deserves hell-fire. So if you are presenting your gift at the altar and suddenly remember that your brother has a grievance against you, leave your gift where it is before the altar. First go and make your peace with your brother; then come back and offer your gift. If someone sues you, come to terms with him promptly while you are both on your way to court; otherwise he may hand you over to the judge, and the judge to the officer, and you will be thrown into jail. Truly I tell you: once you are there you will not be let out until you have paid the last penny.

These verses certainly challenge normal assumptions. There is surely a place for anger on occasion: if the other fellow really has been a fool, a limited show of anger is hardly blameworthy and may even do some good. It is surely reasonable to borrow sometimes: the fact one took a loan from a friend is hardly a reason for missing a religious ceremony! And as for litigation: everyone has a right to go to law, and one would not normally do so if one did not have a reasonable chance of winning. Jesus' observations seem entirely unreasonable. But now let us place them under the heading of 'peacemaking'. It is perfectly true that one has a right to be angry, to accept a loan, to go to law. But it is also true that all these activities are potential sources of conflict, enmity and hatred. They are threats to peace. Peacemakers must therefore renounce even things they have a right to if they are going to make peace their priority and obtain a blessing. It may mean refusing to be angry even when there is good cause to be; returning a loan even when it is willingly given; settling out of court even when one has a good case. In the light of this priority, the usual assumptions cease to hold.

The point of this teaching seems to be well taken by St Paul. In I Corinthians he is rebuking the Corinthian Christians for allowing their community disputes to come before the pagan civil courts. But then it is as if the implication of Jesus' words suddenly flashes through his mind:

You suffer defeat by going to law with one another at all. Why not rather submit to wrong? Why not let yourself be defrauded? But instead, it is you who are wronging and defrauding, and fellow-Christians at that! (I Cor. 6.7–8).

The Christian course is to avoid disputes altogether, even if it means being defrauded and wronged. Why? Because this is the way of the peacemaker, the policy of one who at all costs seeks to put an end to acrimonious dispute and conflict. But this puts peacemaking in a very different class from peacegiving. As we have seen, 'giving peace' depends upon having the necessary power and influence. But *peacemaking* may demand precisely the opposite. It may mean surrendering the social status which allows one to be angry with one's equals or one's inferiors; it may mean diminishing the credit which enables one to obtain a loan; it may mean losing the reputation of a person who wins a law-case and must be respected.

We can now see how 'Blessed are the peacemakers' may

take its place along with the other Beatitudes which sharply challenge our normal assumptions. It is not a simple commendation of those we already respect as dedicated negotiators and mediators. It is a call to make costly sacrifices for the sake of neutralizing the festering consequences of anger, self-righteousness and superiority. It is a challenge to sink one's own interests entirely in order to create peace. This already helps us to see why the peace which Jesus gives cannot be 'as the world gives'. But we must now ask more fundamental questions. What kind of peace does Jesus give? And what is 'peace' anyway?

Peace can be defined as the absence of armed conflict. But few thinkers are ever satisfied with such a negative definition. There may be no war or violence under an oppressive dictatorship; but one would hardly call such a regime 'peace'. In the years following the Gulf War, the United States and Iraq were not actually at war; but it would have been absurd to call their relationship one of 'peace'. The Bible, in any case, uses peace in a far richer sense. It is a state in which there is justice and plenty, in which individuals can pursue their interests without molestation and in which the most precious aspects of family and social life can flourish. But this idyllic state of affairs seldom in fact prevails. Peace, therefore, becomes a symbol of things as they will be in a new and better age.

> How beautiful upon the mountains are the feet of the messenger who announces peace, who brings good news, who announces salvation, who says to Zion, 'Your God reigns' (Isa. 52.7 NRSV).[4]

In this passage 'peace' belongs with good, with salvation, with the reign of God. The words are interchangeable; they all denote that ultimate state of blessedness which God will one day restore to his children. Peace stands for total salvation and redemption. When St Paul speaks of it, he does so in the same breath as he does of life itself (Rom. 8.6).

When the world 'gives peace', it gives a promise of such blessings as are available in the normal way of things. But in the language of religion 'peace' is far more than this. It is the promise of that ultimate salvation to which all human beings look forward. Who can give such a promise? Who is authorized to 'give peace' on these terms? No ordinary messenger. But if God wills the message of peace to be given, he will find a means of doing so. Angels would be suitable; and, sure enough, in Luke's Gospel it is angels who proclaim peace on earth to men of good will (2.14). But certain persons may also have authority to give peace in this deeper, more comprehensive sense (not as the world gives) if they have the power to alter someone's whole life in the direction of salvation. Jesus was such a person. By his power to heal he could say, 'Daughter, your faith has healed you. Go in peace, free from your affliction' (Mark 5.34).

This, then, is the peace which is not as the world gives. It is a reality which belongs to the promised age of the future, but at exceptional times, or by an exceptional person, it may be given or proclaimed even now. We say that even the world's peace involves an element of judgment and of moral discrimination: not all can receive it, and those who give peace must take care on whom they bestow it. The same is true, but to a far greater extent, of peace in its religious dimension. The angels proclaim, 'Peace on earth to all in whom he delights' (Luke 2.14),[5] thereby implying that others cannot receive it. Similarly, as we have seen, when the followers of Jesus give peace to the houses where they wish to stay, the recipients may not be 'worthy' (Matt. 10.13) or 'men of peace' (Luke 10.6), and the peace returns to the donors. Peace involves judgment, it involves discrimination between one person and the next. We can even say: it involves division.

This last observation enables us to approach the paradox presented by an apparently startling saying of Jesus:

> You must not think that I have come to bring peace to the earth; I do not come to bring peace but a sword (Matt. 10.34).

This saying is seized on eagerly by those who seek the authority of Jesus for violent revolutionary activity; but this application is so patently in conflict with Jesus' conspicuous renunciation of violence that we must ask whether the saying has been correctly understood. First, it is important to read on through the following verses:

> I have come to set a man against his father, a daughter against her mother, a daughter-in-law against her mother-in-law; and a man will find his enemies under his own roof (Matt. 10.35–36).

These words are a clear allusion to an oracle of Micah:

> Son maligns father, daughter rebels against mother, daughter-in-law against mother-in-law, and a person's enemies are found under his own roof (Micah 7.6).

As it stands, this is a description of a state of affairs which Jews, with their strong sense of family loyalties, would find abhorrent and alarming. Micah may well have been describing the moral anarchy he experienced in his own time. But his words came to be regarded as a classic description of that period of exceptional disorder and tribulation which was expected to be the immediate forerunner of the New Age. They formed a standard part of the awesome scenario which later prophets and visionaries foresaw as a prelude to the End. They are used even by a sober rabbi who, little more than half a century after Jesus, was convinced of the same necessity for intense suffering and insecurity to precede the establishment of God's kingdom.[6] Why was this necessity felt so strongly? Why must there be this climactic period of tribulation before the End? The clue is probably to be found in the nature of the End itself. What was expected and prayed for was a new age in which God would give unimagined blessings to his faithful people. But this implied judgment: the End could not come until there had been some process of separating out those who were worthy to enter the age to come. And how could this be done? Most people are not ready for a final judgment. They are a mixture of good and bad, their heart is sometimes in one place, sometimes in another. How could a perfectly just God pass a perfectly just judgment on such ambiguous material? Only by subjecting it to severe testing. Place men and women in situations of extreme crisis, and we shall see their true character, we shall know for certain which side they are on. Then judgment can follow with perfect justice; for they will have already judged themselves.

It follows that the promise of the End is like the promise of peace. It implies judgment, separation, division of the sheep from the goats. This suggests a more precise meaning for the 'sword' of which Jesus speaks. In a prophecy of Ezekiel, which is again a scenario of the terrible Last Days, we read that 'men will turn their swords against one another' (38.21). The sword, in this context, is the instrument of division – division in families, division between the just and the wicked. And this, in Luke's Gospel, is exactly how Jesus' saying is understood. For 'sword', Luke writes 'division':

Do you think I have come to give peace on earth? No, I tell you, but rather division (12.51 RSV).

Luke makes another minor change, which makes the point still more clearly. Matthew writes, 'bring peace'. Luke writes, 'give peace',[7] which brings us back to our starting point, the question of peace 'not as the world gives'. Even the world's peace, as we saw, implies a certain element of moral judgment. But Jesus came to give, not that kind of peace, but the true peace which belongs to the New Age, which is withheld from the wicked, and which presupposes God's judgment upon us all – the sword of division. For in Jesus' teaching there is the constant note of urgency and imminence. The kingdom of God, with its essential element of judgment, of discrimination between the good and the bad, the repentant and the obdurate, is at hand. Before it is too late – repent! Otherwise, like Jerusalem itself, you may fail to know 'the way that leads to peace' (Luke 19.42).

We have seen something of the costliness of the peace-making commended by Jesus. It may involve loss of advantage, status, prestige. It is a sacrificial activity. We are now beginning to see also the costliness of peace itself. Even 'as the world gives' there is a sense of having to do with a precious commodity which must not be squandered on those who are unfit to receive it. It demands total dedication, total commitment. It is universally desired; yet its achievement represents one of the greatest challenges that lie before the human race.

2

New Dilemmas

How have Christians responded to this challenge? So far as the absolute priority of peace is concerned, it is probably true to say that they have been less consistent than Jewish thinkers, for whom *shalom* has always represented a value to be striven for even at the expense of compromises with other values.[1] But this is at least partly due to the fact that, unlike the Jews (until recent times), Christians, from the fourth century onwards, have borne some responsibility, not only for peace in the world but also for the maintenance of sound government and justice. Accordingly Augustine (the first major Christian thinker in this area) was not prepared always to give absolute priority to peace: good order and the righting of a wrong might necessitate war, and the question then became, not so much how war could always be avoided, but how the damage it caused could be limited and how the inevitable cost (in terms of human suffering and material resources) could be minimized. So began a tradition of thought known as that of the Just War, which (as we shall see) is based less on Christian revelation than on 'natural law', and which is not even distinctively Christian – it is replicated in almost every respect in Muslim tradition.[2] In the light of this, whatever may have been the case during the first three centuries of Christian history (and the number of Christians who served in armies and the reasons why the majority did not do so are still matters of scholarly debate), the majority of Christians since the time of Constantine has regarded active involvement in war and policing as compatible with the Christian faith, and valued the Just War tradition as a source of guidance in the practical implications of this commitment. But from earliest times there has also been an alternative (and, many would say, more authentic) response: the teaching of Jesus and the whole thrust of the Christian faith has seemed to some to be impossible to reconcile with the bearing of arms or with involvement in any form of violent coercion. As with the Just War tradition, this pacifist stance cannot claim to be distinctively Christian (though it is virtually absent in both Judaism and Islam). The motivation for it may be primarily a sense of revulsion from any form of wounding or killing fellow human beings; or it may be purely pragmatic (war never does any good, indeed it is likely to do more harm than good and make peace and reconciliation the less attainable, therefore any cost is worth paying to avoid it). So by no means all pacifists are Christians. Nevertheless pacifism is a form of witness which is arguably more faithful to Jesus' teaching and example and which is often borne at the cost of great suffering and with a degree of consistency and endurance which challenges the apparent compromise that, at least until now, has been accepted by the Christian majority.

It is important to remember that these two responses to a fundamental aspect of the Christian faith have throughout history virtually never been a major cause of schism or disunity within the Christian church. Even though they might have been thought to raise a crucial matter of doctrine, this has had far less damaging effects on the community of faith (whatever the price paid by some individuals or groups) than many (as it might seem) more trivial theological questions. Both pacifism and non-pacifism have for many centuries been accepted as legitimate responses to the gospel in all but very few churches. There may therefore seem small necessity, and certainly little urgency, to raise the matter afresh. But theology is never static: it is a constant dialogue with the reality with which Christians have to contend in their daily lives. War is no longer what it was when the Just War tradition received its classic formulations. The enormously increased destructiveness of modern weapons and the involvement of whole populations as well as of service men and women create a whole new set of problems for the limitation of warfare by laws and conventions; and new instruments for making and preserving peace between nations (and the increasing problems of controlling violence within nations) offer a new challenge to pacifists as well as to others to admit the legitimacy of the use of force as a last resort to maintain peace. In addition to this, modern biblical study has revealed possibilities for interpreting scripture that were undreamt of in former times. In view of all this the question both of the pacifist option and of the Just War tradition seems to require re-examination.

Let us look first at the problems created since 1945 by the existence of nuclear weapons. New life was given to Just War theorizing, and a new twist to the old argument, by the nuclear debate during the Cold War. Even after Soviet Russia had detonated its own bomb in 1949 and the two Superpowers had settled down to the prospect of indefinite nuclear confrontation, it seemed to many that the advent of nuclear weapons might be the factor which would at last make war an impracticable option for either of them and so provide a new assurance to the world of a lasting peace. If either were to contemplate a nuclear strike on the other it would be met by an equally destructive attack; no sane national leader could contemplate inflicting such destruction on his own country, so hostilities could never begin. Moreover this 'peace' seemed to be obtainable relatively cheaply. The research and the hardware required were of course extremely expensive, but since they would now form the backbone of national defence huge economies could be achieved in conventional armed forces. And in fact nuclear weapons, though expensive, have never accounted for more than a small part of the defence budget of any nuclear power. For a while, peace may have seemed attainable, not only with a certainty seldom known before, but at a price that was comparatively economical.

The illusion did not last long. Quite apart from the psychological and philosophical problems it raised, to which we shall turn in a moment, the technology was found to demand, not a steady state of confrontation with a few massive weapons, but a continual search for superiority in the means both of delivering a surprise attack and of being totally protected from one. However horrific, a policy of 'mutually assured destruction' (as it was officially called for a time) was regarded as the best safeguard against attack; but it was soon realized that it would cease to be effective if the enemy could 'get his retaliation in first' with a pre-emptive strike that would destroy all one's existing missiles. Enormous sums had therefore to be spent in concealing or constantly moving the silos or in developing submarine-launched missiles that would be invulnerable to attack, and also in developing anti-missile defence systems. Moreover it became apparent that massive and indiscriminate bombs would not suffice. Suppose Soviet Russia had used a 'tactical' (allegedly small-scale) nuclear weapon to dislodge part of the Western alliance's defences in Europe. Would it have been credible that the US would launch a missile that would destroy half of Moscow? But if this was *not* credible, deterrence would have failed: the Russians could use their small weapon with impunity. It therefore became necessary to devise a 'graduated' response to every degree in the scale of nuclear attack: each refinement procured by the enemy must be answered with a credible deterrent, not too small to be effective, not too large to be unacceptable as a proportionate response. So began an arms race which followed its course inexorably until the Superpowers were armed with literally tens of thousands of nuclear warheads.

Behind these practical and technological uncertainties lay a daunting number of psychological imponderables and moral dilemmas. The whole theory of deterrence depended on credibility: the enemy must be convinced that the other side would do what it threatened to do in the case of a nuclear attack. But might it be bluffing? And would public opinion, when it came to the point, allow massive retaliation or would it demand a respite for negotiation? Would the chain of command hold? Would a junior officer whose task was essential to carrying out a nuclear strike be willing (in view of the 'Nuremberg principle' that moral responsibility could not be evaded by appealing to 'superior orders') to carry out an action which would certainly cause the death of thousands of innocent civilians? As for the moral dilemmas, help was sought with a new urgency in the Just War tradition. 'Proportionality' was a key criterion: would the destruction caused by a single detonation be in proportion to any possible military advantage achieved? Would a nuclear attack have 'a reasonable prospect of success' if all the likely consequences were taken into account? And did the traditional philosophical theory of 'double effect' help to decide whether the predictable suffering that would be caused to a large number of people (not only at the time but in future generations) would be justified by any advantages gained?

But behind all this lay an argument of a much more fundamental kind. It was not only pacifists who felt a deep revulsion at the idea that it could be part of the official policy of their country to inflict, if need be, incalculable suffering on entire populations. The argument that, under present circumstances, this was the surest way of 'keeping the peace' failed to convince. The threat was there, and indeed was useless unless it was believed that it might be carried out; and countless ordinary citizens felt profoundly unhappy about being party to such a policy or indeed to bearing responsibility for what might turn out to be irreversible damage to the environment with consequences not just for ourselves but for our children and grandchildren. In practical terms such people might not have been able to advance realistic alternatives. By no means all of them were pacifists, in the sense that they would refuse to resort to conventional forms of defence. But all of them had a sense that the stakes were now so high that the decision could not be left to the 'experts' alone. Given the appalling consequences of any nuclear exchange, might it not be better to go for a policy of unilateral nuclear disarmament – the enemy would surely not use nuclear weapons against a non-nuclear power – or at least for a 'no first use' policy despite the Soviet superiority in conventional weapons? Not only the persistent efforts by small groups to blockade and disrupt nuclear installations but the huge marches and protests which took place in several European countries during this period were motivated by a profound sense of moral revulsion against violence inflicted on this scale. This motivation was not far from the traditional springs of pacifism but took on a new form in the light of these new and unprecedented circumstances.

The end of the Cold War seemed for a short time to make these arguments obsolete. The forty-year long confrontation between two nuclear Superpowers, indefinitely stabilized (it seemed) by a policy of mutual deterrence, had suddenly given way to a situation in which the one remaining Superpower and its allies had no adversary capable of launching a major attack or indeed having any motive to do so. The disintegration of the former Soviet Union into independent countries too poor and too politically unstable to pose a realistic threat left the Western alliance with an arsenal far exceeding its needs in any likely contingency, and there was euphoric talk of a 'peace dividend' resulting from a massive reduction in weapons procurement and military establishments. But it soon became apparent that the demise of the Soviet sphere of influence had not necessarily contributed to the peace of the world. The political upheavals in Eastern Europe and the Balkans were liable to erupt into violence and the ever-present threat of turbulence in the Middle East was if anything more difficult to control; and the dismantling and decommissioning of the immense stock of nuclear weapons in Russia and the Ukraine was a task of such political and economic magnitude that it could hardly be assumed to have been accomplished simply by the signing of a treaty. The danger that these impoverished countries might sell their nuclear hardware and expertise to rogue regimes elsewhere became acute. Indeed the nuclear threat, far from having disappeared, was soon seen to have re-emerged in a new form. The danger now was not a major attack on the West by a Superpower but the use of a nuclear weapon by a smaller power or even by a terrorist group that had covertly acquired it and was involved in a local conflict.

The official nuclear powers were now caught in a moral dilemma. The original justification for maintaining a 'nuclear deterrent' – the threat posed by the other side – had now disappeared; moreover the Non-Proliferation Treaty which they had all signed committed them to a progressive reduction of nuclear armaments leading to their total abolition (which was the only ground on which the Pope, representing a massive swathe of Christian opinion, was able to give moral approval to their temporary retention in his message to the UN in 1982). On the other hand it was generally known or at least suspected that other nations had secretly acquired a nuclear capability, in the face of which a credible threat of retaliation might be required at any time; and a country such as Britain, whose permanent seat in the Security Council was becoming difficult to justify apart from its status as a nuclear power, was unlikely to find the political will to renounce its own 'independent' deterrent. As a result the rationale for the legitimate possession of nuclear weapons had shifted. Instead of providing a graduated threat of retaliation in the case of nuclear attack they had become the ultimate sanction lying behind the punitive measures which the international community might use to deprive other nations of the resources to make and maintain any weapons of mass destruction. The necessity of such measures was a significant part of the motivation which led to the Gulf War in 1991 and became the principal factor in the acute tension that developed in subsequent years between Iraq and the United States.

Thus today, at the end of the twentieth century, the simple polarity of East and West having been replaced by a more complex set of international tensions, the hypothetical risk of cosmic disaster implicit in the policy of nuclear deterrence has receded before the more pragmatic necessity to maintain a position of strength from which to restrain and if necessary punish the nuclear ambitions of non-members of the existing nuclear club. The relative complexity of these new circumstances has blunted the edge of the protests mounted by peace movements such as CND – movements in which the energies of many pacifists were deployed. It is hardly conceivable, for instance, that the truly massive anti-nuclear demonstrations which took place in the 1980s could be replicated on anything like the same scale today, even though the substantial reductions which have taken place in the nuclear stock-pile have not appreciably reduced the danger against which the protesters were demonstrating. It is arguable[3] that a strong case can now be made on military as well as moral grounds for the UK to abandon its Trident programme, to renounce the policy of independent nuclear deterrence and so give a lead towards the eventual abolition of all nuclear weapons; but the absence of any immediate nuclear threat has made it difficult to muster massive popular support for this policy, which is perceived by many as one that would weaken Great Britain's power and standing in foreign affairs. Accordingly the attention of the peace movements, including many pacifists, has turned to two related issues: controlling the arms trade and promoting general disarmament.

Campaigns against the arms trade are undertaken from a variety of motives. There is a basic and well-founded fear that the more arms there are in the world the more likely wars are to occur and the more destructive those wars will be. There is grave concern, and sometimes shame, that Britain is now the second largest exporter of armaments in the world and has an economy heavily dependent on their manufacture. There is the international instability caused by the huge stock of weapons purchased by oil-rich countries in the Middle East and the impoverishment inflicted on countries in Africa by arms-hungry dictators. There is the sense of the appalling waste of resources which might have been used to preserve life rather than cause death. There is the danger – of concern also to the military – of weapons falling eventually into the hands of a future enemy. There is the scandal of arms being sold knowingly to oppressive regimes. None of these concerns is distinctively pacifist: they are shared by a very large number of people and have been responded to, in some small measure, by the creation of the UN register of arms transfers, by the European Code of Conduct regulating arms transfers (1998) and by the 'ethical' foreign policy adopted (though somewhat ambivalently) by the present British government. Public revulsion at the export of arms to Indonesia, for example, where they may be used for the subjugation of East Timor, has become a factor which politicians have to take notice of; and it was largely as a result of popular feeling, stimulated by the example of the late Princess Diana, that the British Government has now eliminated its entire stock of anti-personnel landmines. But it has to be said that those who are campaigning for serious reductions in the level of arms transfers have very powerful forces ranged against them. The arms business would mount powerful resistence to reductions in the domestic defence budget. Only a sustained political will to reduce arms exports and to facilitate conversion to the manufacture of civilian goods would make it possible to phase out a substantial part of the industry, and the only country to have achieved this in recent times – Sweden – has a tradition of neutrality that has been quite alien to Britain. And apart from these practical considerations, there remains the absolute right under the UN Charter for any state to defend itself against attack, which implies the right to acquire the weapons needed for this eventuality, which in turn implies the right of other nations to supply them. For these and doubtless other reasons the arms trade is highly resistant to radical attack; campaigners find more fruitful fields of activity in monitoring the quantity of arms transferred to any particular region and the use to which they are or may be put. Such action may well make a significant contribution to the maintenance of peace, and receive the support of pacifists: yet it can hardly be said to form part of a strictly pacifist agenda.

A cause which may seem to further the pacifist project more than campaigning against the arms trade is disarmament. This is a word that holds out great promise, and deserves treatment at somewhat greater length. If nations 'disarm', the threat of war between them, at least temporarily, disappears. They may even lose the power to impose repressive regimes on their own subjects. The announcement of 'Disarmament Talks' in Geneva or Vienna, or of a UN 'Special Session on Disarmament', raises great expectations. In 1961 the General Assembly of the UN unanimously approved a statement that 'efforts should continue without interruption towards the ultimate goal of general and complete disarmament'. For a moment, it seems as if the work of professional negotiators, politicians and diplomats may achieve on behalf of all of us what we all most earnestly desire – peace; and that virtually without cost to any of us. Can this be so?

We shall not find much encouragement in history to think that it can. Nations in the past have 'disarmed'. But they have usually done so in the moment of defeat or victory, under duress from the conquering power or to reduce a level of armament only appropriate in wartime. Or it may be that two nations which once threatened each other, such as France and Britain, no longer have any differences between them such as would make armed conflict worth preparing for. But there is no precedent in history for powerful nations in armed confrontation with one another *voluntarily* initiating 'general and complete disarmament'. At the very least, it would be necessary for all major outstanding causes of conflict to be resolved before such a course could be contemplated.

What in fact is envisaged in 'disarmament' talks at Geneva, Vienna or the UN is of course something much less ambitious. Indeed, those engaged in it use more appropriate language to describe it. Strategic Arms Limitation Talks (SALT), Strategic Arms Reduction Talks (START) – there are many such acronyms, but they are all precise about objectives. Control, limitation, restriction, regulation: these are the aims of all such negotiation; and they have little to do with 'disarmament' in the usually accepted sense. If major nations find themselves locked into an arms race that places an ever increasing burden on their economies, it is to their mutual advantage to agree to 'ceilings' of military equipment that will be observed by both, to areas of military technology that neither side will explore or exploit, to a reduction in stocks of weapons of certain kinds – if this can be done without materially weakening the position of either of them. And if something is of mutual advantage to two nations it ought in principle to be possible for them to reach agreement on it. Of course this may be extremely difficult. Working out equivalence between subtly different strategies or types of weapons, solving the problems of verification and enforcement, and allowing for the complications introduced by other members of an alliance, are tasks that will keep the most skilful and experienced negotiators at work for months if not years. Nevertheless, even in the Cold War there was some success. The Partial Test Ban Treaty of 1963, the Anti-Ballistic Missile Treaty of 1972, and the Intermediate-range Nuclear Force Treaty signed by Gorbachev and Reagan in 1988, were positive steps in the direction of mutually agreed control, and had some effect on military strategy and expenditure. Moreover substantial progress has been made since the Hague Convention of 1907 (banning poison gas and germ warfare) in the Conventions on bacteriological weapons (1972), inhumane weapons (1981), chemical weapons (1993) and landmines (1998). But it is essential to realize that all this, though it represents positive progress, is but a small step towards the declared objective of 'general and complete disarmament'. It is true that under the Conventional Forces in Europe (CFE) Treaty some 50,000 pieces of military hardware (tanks, guns, armoured combat vehicles, combat aircraft and helicopters) from the NATO and former Warsaw Pact countries were destroyed under international supervision in the three years to 1995: this represents genuine progress in disarmament in its technical sense of 'reduction or withdrawal of military forces and weapons'. Yet the remaining stockpile of both conventional and nuclear weapons has a destructive power infinitely greater than anything the world has known before. The admirable objective of 'general and complete disarmament' remains a barely imaginable possiblity.

This is not to say that arms control and reduction have no value beyond saving money. They may not deliver peace, or anything like it, but they do have a certain contribution to make to the well-being and security of the world. This is not perhaps quite the contribution that many people imagine it to be. We are all rightly appalled by the reckless use of the earth's resources to manufacture weapons of destruction when a fraction of the same expenditure could rescue millions from starvation or malnutrition; and it is natural to assume that some reduction in the level of armaments would release resources for aiding the poorer countries of the world. Unfortunately this is extremely unlikely to be the case. It is not even certain that arms control significantly reduces the manufacture of munitions. The armaments industries of developed countries directly or indirectly give employment to many thousands of people. If a certain kind of weapon is to be limited, they will press for diversion of their resources to others. Indeed they constitute one of the most powerful and troublesome lobbies that arms control negotiators are exposed to. But quite apart from this, there is absolutely no evidence that any developed nation would immediately convert a saving in military expenditure into an increase in overseas aid (rather than using it for domestic social purposes). If the rich countries of the northern hemisphere had a serious commitment to helping the south, they would increase their aid budgets tomorrow, without waiting for the outcome of talks on arms control. Conversely, in the present climate success in arms control would be extremely unlikely to make any appreciable difference to the poverty of the Third World.

There is however one benefit of these negotiations which has long-term significance. They may not contribute significantly to reducing the ability of one superpower to inflict crippling damage on another, and they may not make an appreciable difference to the volume of the world's arms production. But the fact that the representatives of nations between which there is potential conflict can agree (when they do) on a complicated treaty of self-limitation in the matter of armaments is in itself a positive contribution to the peace of the world. These negotiations effectively put to the test the confidence of the powerful nations in each other. If they succeed, then they have demonstrated that enough confidence exists for the opposing powers to be able to work out a scheme to their mutual advantage – and other schemes may follow to consolidate the gains already made. Even if they fail, they may have contributed something, in that the expert negotiators will understand their opponents' position better, and the risks of military miscalculation are correspondingly reduced. One of the dangers facing the world at present is a drift into war by a series of accidents. If the leaders of the great powers react hastily to an international crisis, in ignorance of their opponents' real intentions and capabilities, the situation can become intensely dangerous. One of the skills they require has come to be called 'crisis management'. It is a skill towards which arms control negotiations can make a significant contribution. A channel of communication is kept open, and a mass of technical information exchanged, which may be at least as valuable as the existence of a 'hot line' between heads of government.

This is not to say, of course, that a successful round of arms reduction talks may not lead to another, and then another ... until such substantial reductions have taken place that a move towards general disarmament becomes a practical possibility. The Preamble to the Partial Test Ban Treaty of 1963 declared this to be the ultimate objective, and the Non-Proliferation Treaty of 1968 committed the signatories to work not only for nuclear disarmament, but for 'general and complete disarmament under strict and effective international control'. But although these treaties have been undeniably successful in reducing nuclear test explosions and (through the International Atomic Energy Authority, for example) restraining the proliferation of nuclear weapons, any move towards 'general and complete disarmament' appears to be out of reach. And this for good reason. The word 'disarmament' in reality belongs to a different world from 'arms control'. Disarmament alone cannot create peace; and the peace which 'general and complete disarmament' presupposes is of that final character which to many seems simply utopian and which to religious people is part of their ultimate hope. The First World War seemed for a time to be the 'war to end wars'. It was believed that Germany had been so decisively defeated in battle and so thoroughly denuded by reparations that she could never again present a threat to her neighbours. It was believed also that the horrors of modern warfare, as revealed in the carnage of Flanders and Gallipoli, would deter civilized states from ever going to war again. As a result, there was a period of 'general disarmament'. But both beliefs turned out to be false. Germany was allowed to rearm, and twenty years later Europe was again at war. The conditions for 'disarmament' did not exist. 'Peace', in its full sense, had not been established.

Since 1945, we are often told, there has been 'peace'. From the limited view of the European cockpit, this has a measure of truth (or had, until the Balkan crisis of the 1990s). Indeed it is almost unprecedented in history that half a century should have passed without major armed conflict between European states. But Europe is no longer the touchstone of international affairs. World-wide, it is calculated that since 1945 there have been more than a hundred separate wars, often fought by proxy by the Cold War powers who armed local forces. The legacy of these wars, in the availability of small arms and the military culture of the male populations, is with us yet in many parts of Africa. Deaths from these wars have run into tens of millions. In such a world, to suggest that 'general and complete disarmament' is a practical option for any major power, and that it can be rapidly brought about by arms negotiations or by popular disarmament movements, is dangerously unrealistic. Disarmament in this sense presupposes peace – real peace – and is not to be had by such relatively uncostly means. It belongs to that vision of peace which remains alive, despite all discouragements, in the faith of Christians and commits them to pursue those far more costly options which alone are able to draw the world back from the brink of war.

A dramatic illustration of this on a national, as opposed to international, scale is provided by the problems experienced in Northern Ireland over 'decommissioning' weapons after the conclusion of a peace agreement between Unionists and Nationalists. So long as a high degree of fear and distrust continues to be felt between the parties, agreements to surrender arms, however evenly balanced between the former combatants, are difficult to enforce and either side is liable to use the non-compliance of the other as a pretext for breaking the agreement and returning to violent conflict. There could be no better example of the way in which attempts even at limited disarmament can founder in the absence of other conditions necessary for establishing peace. And the same goes for the possession of small arms all over the world. The prevalence of hand guns in the United States certainly contributes to the number of violent crimes committed and will not be seriously reduced until its citizens can be more confident of living at peace with one another. Small arms in Africa have spread like a contagion, and there is no prospect of diminution without an end to tribal warfare. On the other hand a very large number of Swiss men officially retain their rifles after full-time military service, but the state of civic order in that country renders them harmless. Disarmament is seldom a preparation for peace;

it is rather that peace makes it possible either to reduce the number of weapons available or to render them harmless.

But there is another crucial new factor which presents the pacifist both with an opportunity and with a problem. The establishment of international institutions dedicated to maintaining international justice and order has created a world potentially very different from that in which classical Christian thinking on war and peace was formulated, even if the human propensity to violent conflict still seems at times liable to run out of control. In the Preamble to the Charter of the United Nations the member states expressed their determination

> to save succeeding generations from the scourge of War . . . to unite our strength to maintain international peace and security, and to ensure, by the acceptance of principles and the institution of methods, that armed force shall not be used, save in the common interest.

This, of course, was by no means the first time that an attempt had been made to control armed struggle through some form of international institution. Already in the seventeenth century Hugo Grotius (at the cost of personal imprisonment) proposed a regime of international law for the settlement of disputes, and the challenge was taken up in the nineteenth century by a number of dedicated Christian pacifists. Henry Richard, for example, a Welsh nonconformist minister who became a member of parliament in 1868, was instrumental in setting up a peace conference in Paris in 1849 (chaired by Victor Hugo) and succeeded in getting a declaration in favour of international arbitration written into the peace treaty which ended the Crimean War in 1856. A number of Quakers were active in the preparations for the Hague Peace Conference which opened in 1899, but were disappointed that the issue of arbitration took second place to that of arms reduction and control, though somewhat more was achieved in this respect through the intervention of Sir Edward Fry (a Quaker and leader of the British delegation) at the second conference in 1907. It was not until the Covenant of the League of Nations that member states formally accepted an obligation to submit their disputes to the league before resorting to arms – which (in the words of H.A.L. Fisher) was 'as much world-government as the world could stand'.[4] This, of course, did not prevent the Second World War, nor has the United Nations been able to prevent a large number of smaller wars since 1945. For this it is often criticized; but its effectiveness depends entirely on the will of member states to co-operate with it (and indeed to fund it), and by general consent it now (with its various agencies, with the International Court of Justice and soon with an International Criminal Court) represents the world's best hope for the avoidance of war through international arbitration. On these grounds alone it surely deserves the unequivocal support of Christians, pacifist and non-pacifist alike.

There is also a new international strategy in the pursuit of peace which is of importance to the pacifist. The first UN 'peace-keeping' force was deployed in 1956 in Suez. A similar force has been in Cyprus since 1964, in Southern Lebanon since 1978 and in Croatia, Bosnia and Macedonia since 1992. At the time of writing there are sixteen such forces in existence. Their role has been described as 'the projection of the principle of non-violence on to the military plane'.[5] They can be deployed only with the agreement of the countries concerned and may use force only in self-defence or to secure the safe continuance of their mission, and only after all peaceful means of persuasion have been exhausted. Their purpose is to monitor cease fires and peace agreements so as to prevent small incidents from causing a resumption of conflict, to bring stability to an area disturbed

by military action and to contribute to the conditions necessary for a lasting peace. Though the troops are in uniform
and are provided with military vehicles and equipment their
blue berets and white UN transport signify peaceful intentions and the deliberate renunciation of the use of force. As
such, they represent a form of action and service which
may be claimed to be consistent with the commitment to
non-violence which many feel to be implied by the practice
of the Christian religion.

Yet this form of peace-keeping also presents pacifists with
a problem. Many peace-keeping soldiers are unarmed; but,
if not, they are permitted to use their weapons as a last
resort, whether to resist attack on themselves or to enable
their work to continue. For this reason a consistent pacifist
would necessarily have to withhold approval: the activity
of peace-keeping, if strenuously resisted, may always
develop into armed conflict. The rules of engagement under
which UN personnel may operate are stringently drawn,
but the use of weapons can never be totally excluded. In the
eyes of some Christians, therefore, a peace-keeping force
cannot qualify as a valid expression of Christian non-violent
principles. But in fact this is only a particular instance of a
more general dilemma. In the past, 'keeping the peace' was
seen as a prime objective of diplomacy; and the preferred
means of achieving it was by maintaining, through alliances
of armed states, a balance of power sufficient to deter the
aggressive intentions of any of them. This strategy, since it
relied explicitly on the threat of military action, was clearly
incompatible with a pacifist position, and Christians who
believed themselves committed to non-violence necessarily
dissociated themselves from it and objected to the concen-
trations of armaments which it required. Today the concept
of a balance of power is less in evidence. It has been partly
displaced, not only by economic alliances which greatly
reduce the risk of war between the partners and may develop

(as in Europe since 1945) into a community of nations with a shared commitment to democracy, human rights, the rule of law and market economics; but by international institutions intended to facilitate the settlement of disputes without armed conflict and to restrain acts of aggression by various forms of non-violent dissuasion. The aim, certainly, is to create a world in which the pacifist will feel more at ease: the efforts being made today to make war obsolete, and so to make possible a consistent commitment to non-violence, are arguably greater than at any time in the past. But the dilemma arises precisely because war so evidently has not been abolished. International law and international policing continue to be defied by rulers and states intent on achieving their national aims by any means available to them, and the international community has found itself impelled to use force to restrain them. The solution is sometimes proposed by pacifists of placing battalions of disciplined but unarmed civilians in the path of violent and aggressive forces. It is true that in the Philippines, for example, crowds of up to 100,000 unarmed people effectively kept the 'rebel' army and the Marcos' army apart for four days in February 1986 until Marcos resigned – the tank crews refused to advance over the bodies of people at prayer.[6] But in other cases (such as the admittedly small number of OSCE observers in Kosovo in January 1999) a civilian presence may be ineffective or even simply succeed in creating a human shield preventing others from restraining an aggressor. We shall explore this question of 'non-violent action' further in chapter 5. But, for the time being at least, it remains true that, as with UN peace-keeping forces, so with all attempts to ensure compliance with the terms of the UN Charter, it seems impossible to avoid the threat of military action as a last resort. The dilemma for pacifists is that they cannot easily condone the use of this ultimate sanction; yet how are they conscientiously to dissociate themselves from the development of international institutions of which the prime purpose is to forestall serious disputes or to settle them without recourse to force, and which arguably represent the most serious attempt ever made to restrain the persistent warlike tendencies of human kind?

3

The Ambiguity of Scripture

It is well known that, when appeal is made to the Bible, both pacifists and non-pacifists are able to find texts and narratives which support their position. But it is also evident that the Old Testament is a good deal more recalcitrant to being used in the pacifist cause than the New. In the Hebrew scriptures there is no doubt whatever that God is a God of battles, a God who 'goes out with our armies' – a theology which has given great reassurance to the leaders of countless military enterprises who have confidently proclaimed that God was on their side. No amount of sophisticated modern criticism can materially alter the overall impression given by these scriptures of a God who approves the use of force and is often invoked as the champion and protector of armed forces. So much is generally agreed; but it is important to set this finding in the larger context of the biblical under-standing of the human situation and our relationship with God. In this area there have certainly been some advances in biblical interpretation. Let us begin with the story of the Fall.

The story of the 'Fall' in Genesis 2–3 – that is, the creation of Adam and Eve to enjoy a blessed state in the garden of Eden, their act of disobedience and their expulsion from the garden – causes trouble to the modern interpreter on at least two grounds. In the first place, even if the story is not regarded as in any sense historical but rather as a mythical or poetic representation of the human predicament, it is difficult to reconcile with any understanding of humanity which takes seriously (as we must) our evolutionary origins. We now know beyond all doubt, in a way that the biblical writers could not know, that human beings have evolved from lower to higher and have progressed from barbarism to various forms of civilization. The notion of a golden or paradisal age from which we have actually declined flies in the face not only of our ascertainable pre-history but also of a stubborn conviction that, despite constant reverses, the upward direction can be maintained, yielding still undreamt of possibilities for peace, prosperity and social living. In the second place it seems to locate the cause of the trouble in the personal pride, ambition and consequent disobedience of individual men and women. No one can deny that it is indeed precisely these proclivities which cause a great deal of the misery by which we are still surrounded; to this extent the story offers a telling analysis of the human condition. But today, in an age when the greatest sufferings of the innocent are caused, not by individual sinfulness, but by the ruthless exercise of power by violent and aggressive regimes, the biblical account seems to have little purchase on the realities with which many of us have to wrestle.

At least part of these difficulties may be due to our assumption that the story ends with the expulsion from Eden at the end of chapter 3. But the biblical narrative continues without any apparent break into the story of Cain and Abel, and so furnishes us with a vital component for understanding what we have come to call the 'Fall'. From an evolutionary perspective the biblical account might now run like this. At the moment of emerging from and distancing themselves from their animal forbears, human beings evolved a will independent of their creator. This independence (explained by Jewish interpreters as a voluntary and deliberate withdrawal by God to leave room for the beings he had created and endowed with free will) was accompanied from the first by 'the knowledge of good and evil'. This knowledge manifested itself in a distinctively human form of behaviour. Whereas the evolutionary progress of all other species had been effected by the 'survival of the fittest', weaklings being necessarily allowed to perish, the emergence of self-consciousness in human beings was apparently accompanied by the opposite: they nursed and cared for their most vulnerable. They saw it to be 'evil' to ignore the sufferings of the weak, and embraced the 'good' of providing for the survival of other than the fittest.

But alongside this distinctive and decisive advance occurred another development with profound consequences for human behaviour. For no better reason than the apparent unfairness with which all living beings are treated by the environment to which they have to adapt (and so, in a sense, by God) Cain killed his brother Abel, so initiating a pattern of violence that would far exceed one-for-one retaliation: Cain's death would be avenged seven-fold, Lamech's seventy-seven-fold (4.15,24). Unlike virtually any other species, humans became beings who would wage war on one another in large numbers and to the death. Twenty thousand British soldiers killed in one day in the Battle of the Somme, sixty-six thousand Japanese civilians incinerated in a few seconds or consigned to a lingering death in Hiroshima and Nagasaki, were not freakish aberrations of a normally pacific human nature; they were merely exceptional instances, made possible for the first time by modern technology, of a typically human proclivity. The biblical writer was correct to include the murder of Abel and its lethal consequences in his analysis of the human predicament. In the light of it, theology can meaningfully speak of a 'fall'. The evolution of human beings into creatures uniquely endowed with a sense of right and wrong (distinctively manifested in their care for other than the fittest) was accompanied by the development of a characteristic virtually confined to their species: a tendency to internecine warfare.

How has this distinctively human belligerent instinct been prevented from causing widespread destruction and the virtual extermination of populations? Certain prudential considerations have always influenced military ambitions. 'What king will march to battle against another king, without first sitting down to consider whether with ten thousand men he can face an enemy coming to meet him with twenty thousand?' (Luke 14.31). A reasonable prospect of success was always, and is still, essential to any warlike venture. Fortunately, conditions for this are not frequently present. The military posture of one nation evokes military preparedness in others, powerful empires have rivals, small nations join defensive alliances. A 'balance of power' has been an unquestioned goal of peaceful diplomacy until this century and has arguably prevented a large number of wars (though by no means all). A further restraint has been the need for morale on the battlefield. Mercenaries may be willing to risk their lives for their pay; but a national army, if it is to fight effectively, requires public support at home, strongly favourable coverage in the media and the motivation of a clearly-grasped objective, such as the defence of their own territory or the punishment of a dangerous aggressor. The whims of a dictator are not so easily carried into effect by war unless supported by a strong ideology. In short, an instinct for self-preservation exercises a powerful restraint on the warlike tendencies of peoples and their rulers.

A further prudential constraint on belligerency is relatively recent: the greatly increased destructiveness of modern weapons. The threat which is posed to entire populations, if not to humanity itself, by any outbreak of large-scale war has provoked the international community into defining more narrowly the purpose for which any nation may deliberately go to war. Whereas the Just War tradition envisaged the righting of a wrong as a legitimate reason for declaring war, and defined the condition of 'just cause' accordingly, the UN Charter allows only for self-defence as a legitimate ground for active hostilities, and even that only as a temporary measure pending the settlement of the dispute by international arbitration. The effectiveness of this limitation has of course depended on the willingness of the international community to enforce it: in the case of the Soviet invasion of Afghanistan or the Israeli conquest of the West Bank, not at all; in the case of the Iraqi invasion of Kuwait, to a considerable degree – though in this case it is plausibly argued that some members of the alliance formed under UN auspices were acting as much for reasons of self-interest as to enforce a principle of the UN Charter. However this may be, the Charter is evidence for an international consensus that the only justifiable reason for going to war is self-defence – a principle which, if observed by every member state, should logically put an end to all but civil wars. This represents a notable advance in Just War theory, in that it narrows the notion of 'just cause' down to the single issue of self-defence, even though the enforcement of it may involve other nations (as in Kuwait) to commit their forces to an operation that could be described in traditional terms as 'righting a wrong'. Indeed the international consensus extends further than this. Reprisals have long been regarded as illegal. But military operations undertaken for purposes of retaliation have been regarded as justifiable, and still are by some nations. Competent international authorities have now begun to move towards declaring these also to be illegal.[1] Again, the effectiveness of such a ruling would depend on the willingness of members of the UN to observe it or enforce it; but this development itself it is a notable sign of the continuing search for means to curb those belligerent impulses which are the curse of Cain.

At any rate, whether this tendency to internecine warfare is a genuine inherited characteristic of human beings, a product of social and cultural conditioning, or a combination of both (a question vigorously debated by socio-biologists today), we can follow the author of Genesis to the extent of describing the human predicament as a perpetual conflict between two instinctive and incompatible tendencies: on the one hand to go to great lengths caring and providing for the weak, on the other to expose the strong (and if necessary the weak also) to the risk of sudden death or prolonged suffering through acts of warfare. On one day considerable resources, supported by a wave of public concern, will be devoted to saving the life of a yachtsman lost at sea; on another, still greater resources, again supported by public opinion, will be committed to destroying an enemy battleship with the possible loss by drowning of a thousand men. One of the recurrent tasks and occasional achievements of civilized endeavour has been to foster the first of these instincts and to restrain the second.

If we ask what contribution religion has made to these tasks and achievements it must be said that the Hebrew scriptures show vastly more concern for the first than for the second. Protection of the weak, the poor and the vulnerable from the depredations of the influential rich is the distinguishing mark of the justice of God, and is a constant of the teaching of both the law and the prophets. It is indeed the religious basis for the broad consensus which exists today in support of universal human rights: it is the protection of the weak and the restraint of the strong which is the object of all human rights conventions rather than the preservation of life at all costs. To this extent the Hebrew scriptures may be said to have had a profound, if indirect, effect on modern civilization. But in respect of the second task, that of limiting the incidence and restraining the brutality of war, the same scriptures have singularly little to offer. The Hebrews were no less warlike than their neighbours, the approval of God was often sought and usually assumed for their campaigns, and their treatment of the vanquished, allegedly enjoined upon them by God, sometimes exceeded in ruthlessness that of their enemies. As a small nation, surrounded first by belligerent tribes (some of whom it had actually displaced) and subsequently by powerful empires, its strategic aims were the integrity of its territory and the extirpation of foreign cults and practices (if necessary by the extermination of entire communities); its tactics often favoured attack as the best means of defence; divine support for its armies was thought to be demonstrated by astonishing victories against apparently insuperable odds; its defeats, which seemed unaccountable to the psalmist, were attributed by both prophets and chroniclers, not to the illegitimacy of the military engagement, but to the social, moral and religious failings of the nation.

But more than this: it is not just that in matters of war the Hebrews seem to have been no better than their contemporaries in other cultures; in some respects they seem to have been even less humane, and to have believed that God endorsed their brutality. For example, it was often seen as a condition of God's support of their army that the taking of a town to which they laid claim for future occupation should be followed by the total extirpation of the inhabitants in order to avoid any possible contamination by pagan religious practices; indeed the approval of God is claimed for the massacre or enslavement of the inhabitants of captured cities even when there is no intention to occupy the site (Deut. 20.10 – 14). When Jerusalem was captured by a pagan nation in 598 BCE its treatment was arguably more humane than that which the Jews believed themselves to be authorized by their scriptures to inflict on their defeated enemies.

There is, it is true, an important passage in the prophet

Amos which seems to promise the punishment of God for actions contrary to the normal laws of war – inhumane weapons, the deportation of populations, treacherous murder and the massacre of women and children (Amos 1.3–2.3). But in this denunciation of foreign countries Amos is not appealing to the justice of God as revealed in his own scriptures but apparently to something like a 'natural law' which could be held to apply universally.[2] By contrast, the standard of warlike conduct apparently set by the God of the Hebrews was uncompromisingly ruthless, and caused a problem even in antiquity. When the Jewish historian Josephus was summarizing for his Gentile readers the rules of military engagement contained in Deuteronomy chapter 20,[3] he evidently found it necessary to make them sound more humane. The biblical text simply commands the Israelites to parley before laying siege to a town, offering the inhabitants the alternatives of total destruction or safe conduct into slavery; Josephus dilutes the force of this by representing all Jewish wars as essentially defensive and suggests that the parley could have been understood as a serious offer of peace. Rather similarly, modern interpreters, dismayed by the fact that God appears to be credited with authorizing these uncivilized military tactics, tend to invoke the explanation that at times the Israelites believed themselves to be engaged in a 'Holy War' which required the extermination of any possible source of pagan influence in a territory that had been conquered by force of arms. Failure to ensure the purity of the land of Israel by allowing alien elements to persist within its borders constituted a serious sin and could attract divine retribution. The positive side of this ideology was the reliance it encouraged on the divinely supported morale of the army. God might manifest his approval of their campaign by affording them victory in the face of overwhelming numbers, or he might even cause them deliberately to reduce their own forces in order to give clear proof of the supernatural power at work on their side. It was perhaps this readiness to rely on divine help in the battlefield which caused them to allow liberal exemptions from military service to those who were starting a farm, building a house, or getting married. Even those who showed fear or cowardice were exempted. But none of this materially alters the impression gained from these scriptures as a whole of a God who is content that his people should use military force with considerable ruthlessness and brutality.[4]

A possible escape route from this quandary is offered by the fact that the New Testament clearly does not endorse everything in the Old. Commandments concerning the ritual in the Temple, for example, are made obsolete by the new dispensation of a 'temple not made with hands'. Moreover there are other strands in the Old Testament which present God as merciful and not vengeful, as summoning to peace rather than war, as caring for the world and not just the people of Israel – and it is these and not the harsher strands that are seen by Christians to presage and authenticate the person of Jesus as the Christ. And in any case was not Jesus a 'new Moses'? Did he not have authority to repeal or reform the ancestral laws? 'It was said in old time ... but I say unto you' – is this not a clear statement of Jesus' authority to supersede the Law of Moses with his own ethic? To a certain extent this may be true – though even this set of sayings in the Sermon on the Mount is probably an instance of Jesus *re-interpreting* rather than repealing or reforming the existing law. For how, in practical terms, could he have done otherwise? The Law of Moses was administered up and down the country in courts consisting of men well versed in it, following a traditional school or schools of interpretation and skilled in applying it to contemporary situations. How could a single teacher introduce totally new legislation, or even a totally new style of interpretation, into such a well-established system? Moreover Jesus consistently referred to the Hebrew scriptures as possessing divine authority. His vocation cannot have been to introduce new laws, but rather to offer an interpretation which would invest its provisions with a radically new moral force.

Given, therefore, that there are no recorded instances of Jesus rejecting or correcting any of the Old Testament passages relating to warfare, and given also that (in the view of many scholars) Jesus was not in the business of revising the Law of Moses anyway, it is hard to argue that his silence on these matters suggests disapproval or an intention to introduce a new ethic for war. A more fruitful approach may be to allow for some development in the Hebrews' understanding of God. Did they perhaps simply grow out of their early belligerency? It is certainly true that the passages which apparently authorize strikingly inhumane military procedures are relatively early and belong to a period when similar conduct was taken for granted in the surrounding cultures. Later texts make no mention of them; and if these are regarded as more authoritative (because more recent and 'developed'), then the earlier and more disturbing texts may be disregarded as obsolete. But this is an argument which relies dangerously on silence: it is not that the later texts contradict the bellicosity of the earlier ones, they make no reference to warfare at all; and the reason for their silence cannot be presumed to be disapproval, given that the situation of the Jews when they were written was one in which no military campaign was any longer conceivable (and in the brief period when it was – that of the Maccabees – there is little sign of any softening of the will to punish the enemy). Indeed by the time of Jesus it is fair to say that the whole question had become academic. The Jewish population of Palestine was under Roman occupation and was forbidden to carry arms except under the orders of Roman officers. In these circumstances, neither Jesus nor (so far as we know)

his learned contemporaries had any occasion to make a
direct comment on the martial tradition found in the
Hebrew scriptures. We can hardly infer from their silence
that they utterly disapproved of it. Indeed in the case of
Jesus the evidence seems to point in the opposite direction.
He nowhere explicitly condemns the institution of war, he
converses with a Roman soldier without making any criticism of his profession and on one occasion he apparently
sanctions the carrying of weapons (Luke 22.36–38) in a
way which seems hardly compatible with a total abhorrence
of every form of violent action.

On the other hand, of course – and this is the real strength
of the pacifist case – we have sayings of Jesus which seem
to rule out the use of force in conflict altogether. 'Do not
resist evil', 'Turn the other cheek', 'Agree with your adversary quickly' – these words from the Sermon on the Mount
recommend an ethic which appears to be totally opposed
to violence in any form. Placed alongside the equally radical
and indeed (in that culture or any other) unprecedented
command to 'Love your enemies', they seem to exclude
altogether the option of personal retaliation against violent
attack and so, by implication, any involvement in military
(or, for that matter, guerilla or 'Zealot') action. If these
words could be taken at their face value and assumed to
apply to all situations of violence in which Christians of
today might find themselves there would seem to be no
question that Christianity is a pacifist religion and that every
Christian must be willing to endorse an absolute renunciation of the use of violent means of coercion.

Unfortunately the matter is not so simple. The teaching
of Jesus is not expressed in the form of timeless truths and
axioms which may be assumed to apply to any situation at
any time. For the most part the Gospels preserve it in
particular contexts which give it a specific application and
meaning. Moreover these contexts are not historically

secure: modern critical scholarship is well aware that the sayings of Jesus were remembered more accurately than the context in which they were spoken, and the occasion for each may well have been forgotten by the time the Gospels came to be written. The evangelists may therefore have had to devise whatever context seemed best to fit the saying in question – and there are instances where this has undoubtedly been the case, reflecting the later interests of the church rather than any possible situation in which Jesus may actually have found himself. The problem with the sayings with which we are concerned is that they occur for the most part in the Sermon on the Mount (or the equivalent 'Sermon on the Plain' in Luke) which is clearly a discourse compiled from a collection of Jesus' teachings that had long lost the original context in which they were spoken. But it remains true that the greater part of his teaching in the Gospels is related to particular persons and situations, and we must assume that the same was originally the case for the material in the 'Sermon'. In which case it is necessary to ask what their particular target is likely to have been; and the sequence of sayings concerning a blow on the cheek, a requisition by the occupying authorities to go a mile's journey, the theft of a coat and the threat of legal action seem to belong firmly within the sphere of personal attitudes and responses and fall far short of any situation involving armed combat (though they may well illustrate appropriate behaviour for a subject in an occupied country and can be interpreted as examples of the way in which the underdog may take the initiative away from the oppressor.)[5] They can hardly be assumed to be relevant to the question whether one may risk causing injury or death in defence of the innocent against attack or whether it is permissible to wage war for a just cause. If Jesus said anything on these wider issues it has not been recorded; and we cannot lightly assume that what was intended to apply to personal behaviour in the face of insult or injustice has direct relevance to more general questions of peace and war.[6]

A further complication is introduced by the style of Jesus' teaching. One of its distinctive features is a tendency towards at times almost grotesque exaggeration in order to emphasize a point. A camel attempting to pass through the eye of a needle, a plank of wood in one's eye preventing one from seeing the speck of dust in someone else's, an offering (presumably of a live bird or animal) abandoned in the Temple precincts while one searches someone out in the back streets of Jerusalem – these and many more contribute to the impression of a teacher who by no means always expected to be taken literally. So what about the radical moral commands to love our enemies, to give away everything we possess, to look for no repayment of our loans and place no limit on our generosity and concern? Are these to be complied with literally, or are they instances of Jesus giving distinctive force to his teaching by a touch of exaggeration? This is by no means merely a technical question of biblical scholarship. As we shall be reminded in a later chapter, Christian responses to Jesus' radical teaching on, for example, personal possessions have ranged from the absolute self-impoverishment of Francis of Assisi to the charitable benefactions of successful business men. Similarly, it cannot be assumed that teaching on personal non-violence and non-retaliation was intended to be slavishly adhered to in every possible situation. One who is absolutely committed to abandon self-defence for himself in response to Jesus' command 'not to resist evil' may nevertheless feel that it would be taking this teaching further than it was intended to go if he were to refuse to defend his family or even his country from attack.

In the course of the last century biblical scholarship has come up with still more recondite means by which the apparent import of Jesus' radical teaching may be evaded. The view of Albert Schweitzer, for example, was that Jesus was convinced of the early end of the world and that his moral teaching was therefore intended merely as an 'interim ethic', hardly applicable to the circumstances of an obstinately continuing world order. Though no longer widely accepted in the form in which he propounded it, this view nevertheless continues to exert some influence. Some scholars, for example, regard the radical teaching in the Sermon on the Mount as evidence for an early ascetic sect within the Christian community whose teaching found its way into the 'Jesus tradition' but need not now command our allegiance. Others regard the original teaching as so deeply conditioned by the particular circumstances in which it was given and the particular audience to whom it was addressed that it is by definition inapplicable to the totally different circumstances of today. Even without adopting a definite position on these questions one is forced to agree that these sayings cannot be claimed to give clear and unqualified direction to a Christian of today in matters relating to peace and war.

But it is not on the strength of individual sayings that the Christian pacifist case is principally founded. A far more solid basis exists in the conduct of Jesus himself when confronted by violent forces and in the centrality of non-resistant suffering at the heart of Christian doctrine. Indeed the right place to start may be with the crucifixion. It is common ground among Christians that this was an act of God bringing about the redemption of the world through the willing sacrifice of his Son for the sins of all. But was not the crucifixion in some sense also exemplary? Certainly the command of Jesus (Mark 8.34) to 'take up our cross' (whatever its precise origin and meaning[7]) suggests that our conduct should be in some way likened to Jesus' final act of self-offering, and when Paul speaks of 'being crucified with Christ' (Gal. 2.20) and of 'completing what is lacking in Christ's sufferings' (Col. 1.24) he is clearly envisaging a course of personal discipleship which includes the willing acceptance of suffering rather than some form of resistance to it. The most frequent phrase used in the New Testament to describe the crucial event of our salvation is that Jesus was 'handed over' (indeed in one instance there is the strange statement that Jesus 'handed himself over' (I Peter 2.23)). If our discipleship is a matter of following Jesus right up to and including a willingness to 'take up his cross' then it must include the same willingness to be 'handed over' – that is, to offer no resistance.

It may be that we can go further. If the crucifixion is a demonstration, not only of God's love for human kind in offering his Son, but of his very nature as revealed in Christ, then we may read off from it a parable of God's approach to the whole phenomenon of violence and evil. Deep in human nature, it may be said, is the urge to get what we want, if necessary by violence. If we are frustrated in this aim, or if we feel guilty at not achieving it, we shall seek to satisfy ourselves by victimizing the person we hold responsible for our failures or our difficulties; and this may result in that person's expulsion from our society (which, for this purpose, we define as including only people like ourselves) or even death. Thus, whatever the unconscious drive which leads us to identify and punish a scapegoat, we rationalize our aggression by believing that the victim's conduct has been so evil that it justifies our action. This human pattern is contradicted at every point by the 'handing over' and crucifixion of Christ. God is identified, not with our punitive urge towards self-justification, but with the victim of it; and the resurrection shows this acceptance of the infliction of force, instead of resistance to it, to be the way in which God releases and extends the influence of his love in the world. If we are to 'take up our cross' and 'be crucified with Christ' it would seem to follow that we are called unequivocally to adopt the same stance of absolute non-resistance to violent assault and to meet our enemies and attackers with the forces only of persuasion and love.

This is a powerful argument, and clearly places the onus of defence on those Christian non-pacifists who nevertheless believe it to be compatible with their faith if necessary to take up arms – as indeed the majority of Christians have done since at least the fourth century. But before we attempt to answer it we need to define more precisely the area to which this argument applies. A willingness to 'suffer with Christ' is not the same as 'passive resistance'. There is no hint in the Bible or in the early formulation of Christian doctrine that Christ's willingness to be 'handed over' and die for us was seen as a means of actually restraining the violence of others. The unresisting death of Christ is presented, not as the ultimate cost of a consistently pacifist stance, but as a sacrifice freely accepted in obedience to the will of God. His followers also may carry the cross, with its cost of unmerited suffering or even death; but (in Paul's understanding, for example) such discipleship is a means of 'crucifying the self' and achieving a close identification with Christ and his saving work. Nowhere in the New Testament is the crucifixion represented as a pattern of non-violent action to achieve a particular temporal end or as a means for restraining the violence of others. It is a sign of the willingness to 'lose one's life in order to save it', and implies a refusal to retaliate against evil and violence in any form. It may lead the Christian to be a 'peacemaker' through patient and costly mediation but not to seek to separate the parties by 'non-violent' intervention; it implies a deliberate, if vulnerable, standing aside from the conflict but not an attempt to restrain it – impartial ambulance work rather than 'non-violent' identification with a cause. Above all, it is a divinely authenticated sign that the God of Christian belief is a God of persuasion, not of coercion.

The question at issue, therefore, is not whether a Christian should adopt a posture of 'non-violence' or 'passive resistance' in response to the principles of the Christian faith (this will be discussed later on) but whether the willing acceptance of suffering which seems to be implied in Christian discipleship precludes the use of force to defend oneself, one's family or one's country. To this question it has to be said that the response of Jesus' followers has been ambivalent right from the beginning. Willing suffering for the sake of Christ, even to the point of death, is both recommended and recorded by New Testament writers; but at the same time the power of the sword which sustained the Roman provincial administration, though regarded as demonic in the Book of Revelation, is acknowledged to be according to the will of God by St Paul. Just as centurions appear in both the Gospels and Acts, and are accorded respect without explicit criticism of their profession, so in the early centuries it is impossible to affirm that no Christians were willing to bear arms; indeed in the second century, under Marcus Aurelius, the Twelfth Legion is known to have contained a large number. Even St Martin, after his baptism, served in the army for two further years.[8] Moreover those who refused military service were motivated not only, if at all, by a revulsion from physical violence: they feared also the contagion of immorality and licence which was permitted to the military on active service, and they were aware of the pressure to conform to the emperor cult and other pagan practices, which in times of persecution could result in exposure and even cost them their lives.[9] Even when this threat was removed in the fourth century and idolatrous worship abolished, there were still those who refused service on the grounds of their Christian faith, though the majority of Roman soldiers were soon to become baptized Christians. Meanwhile, by the end of the fourth century, Augustine was arguing that the commandment, 'Thou shalt not kill', did not apply to the soldier or the magistrate so long as they

were acting under proper authority for the establishment
and maintenance of justice. Indeed it was not until relatively
modern times that a recognizably 'pacifist' response to their
religion began once again to be adopted by a substantial
minority of Christians.

This is not to say that the majority has been either faithless
or uncaring (though ventures such as the Crusades and institutions such as the Inquisition pose awkward questions for
the Christian apologist). On the contrary, a great deal of
Christian thought and energy have been devoted to preventing and limiting violent conflict, though retaining the
option to engage in it if all else fails. As we have seen, this
enterprise – the Just War tradition – cannot easily be based
on the Hebrew or Christian scriptures: the first show little
interest in limiting the severity of war, the second yield virtually nothing which is relevant. Instead, theorists have had
recourse to a philosophical tradition with its roots in classical antiquity and its classic formulation in terms of Natural
Law. This tradition still has its advocates today, and indeed
enjoyed something of a revival in discussions of the justification for the Gulf War in 1991. But it is at least arguable
that new factors have emerged which require this tradition
to be radically revised, if not abandoned altogether. This
will be the subject of the next chapter.

4

The Just War Tradition Today

The roots of Just War thinking are to be found, not in scripture, but in the Stoic tradition of philosophy that can be traced back in its essentials to Aristotle. The highest priority was not (as it tends to be in modern thinking) the preservation of human life, or even innocent life, at all costs. Life was not regarded in the ancient world as universally precious, and in the Christian religion was in any case regarded as only a preparation for the life to come; therefore its preservation was of value mainly as an opportunity for repentance and growth in sanctity. The evil of war was seen less in terms of its cost than of the licence it gave for the exercise of unruly passions and desires: 'love of violence, revengeful cruelty, fierce and implacable enmity, wild resistance and the lust for power and such like'.[1] These passions exist, and war may be necessary to curb them and restore justice and order; but the means to be used should be those approved by reason and informed by virtue. Hence the familiar Just War principles governing the conditions under which war may be initiated (*jus ad bellum*) and waged (*jus in bello*). There is nothing distinctively Christian about these: they result more from common sense and rational inference than from religious revelation, and are assented to by members of other religions and by secular thinkers. But, in its Christian formulation, Just War thinking as we have inherited it from Augustine and Aquinas represents a delicate balance between divine revelation and natural law. Aquinas in particular sees the natural law as both authoritative in its own right, because it is a system of ethical rules which anyone can understand and accept simply on account of being endowed with human 'nature'; and yet as totally dependent upon God, since God makes all the kinds of creatures there are, including human kind which has this nature and is thus gifted with a capacity for moral responsibility. For Aquinas it is impossible to believe in natural law without, at least implicitly, believing in God as its author.

Now from our twentieth-century vantage-point we can see how delicately poised was the mediaeval bridge on which Aquinas stood, linking revelation and reason, divine command and natural law. On the one hand, belief in human nature as God's creation was not just a philosophical or theological postulate: it was embedded as a founding element of the political and economic culture of mediaeval Europe. Wars between Christian princes, for example, were commonly regarded as subject to regulation by divinely authorized *natural* laws. These provided the means for distinguishing (say) lawful from unlawful authority, or just from unjust causes, for going to war. On the other hand crusades against the infidel could not be regulated by such laws, for they were holy wars, waged at divine command. Consequently the natural rights to which Christian enemies were entitled were not to be conceded to infidel enemies, who were fighting against God's explicit command and who did not belong to Christendom.[2] Thus (to take one notorious case) it was forbidden to Christian soldiers, by the second Lateran Council in 1139, to use the cross bow against Christian enemies.[3] But its use against the infidel was not forbidden by this decree.

We recognize the fragility of the Thomist bridge when we look further ahead, to the sixteenth century. Whereas

Aquinas' Just War theory 'hardly envisages cultures in which Christ has not explicitly been preached at all',[4] Franciscus Vitoria (1480–1546) had to confront this problem head-on. He was the first significant Christian theologian faced with having to apply Just War criteria to wars waged by Christians against people who had never had any contact with Christianity. The Spanish wars against the American 'Indians' were not 'crusades' commanded by God; and, unlike the crusaders, the *conquistadores* were certainly not motivated by obedience to the demands of confessors that they should undertake penance. Here then was a new puzzle: how to apply the natural criteria for justice in war when there was no shared Christian culture available to both sides. The puzzle was soluble in the end only by cutting the link between natural law and belief in a divinely instituted common Christian culture. Despite Vitoria's valiant efforts to keep alive the Thomist marriage of divinely revealed law with nature, in the end divorce became inevitable. In the work of Grotius and his successors,[5] Just War theory was secularized precisely in order to deal with situations which involved people quite unfamiliar with Christianity. Natural law now aspired to be autonomous and to provide the basis for an international law that would hold equally for peoples of all races and cultures. The 'body' (*sōma*) of Thomist natural law, dependent as it was on God as its alpha and omega, had become the mere 'flesh' (*sarx*) of a legal order operating on its own. Thenceforward the problem would always be how to prevent this flesh from becoming mere grass.[6]

Now of course, the system of autonomous international law which we have inherited from this divorce is of inestimable practical value. In it lies today's hope for a more peaceful, humane world in which conflict can be conducted without violence. Our hope is for an international law which breaches the cultural walls which divided Christendom from the pagan or infidel world. Today, legally enforceable rights are claimed to belong to everybody, irrespective of religion, race, gender or whatever, simply because we are all human.

Yet, as we know, the bridge between cultures on which modern international law stands is at least as fragile as that on which Aquinas stood. An example will illustrate this point. It is drawn from the work of the International Court of Justice.[7] On 8 July 1996 this Court gave its advisory opinion on the legality (or otherwise) of the use or threat of use of nuclear weapons. It emerged that international law, thus interpreted by the only authoritative judicial body in the world, cannot quite make up its mind on the crucial issue of nuclear use and nuclear disarmament. For the product of its deliberations taken as a whole is ambivalent – as the international judges from different countries and cultures have shown by their divergent interpretations of its meaning.[8] This is perhaps not surprising when we reflect that although the judges of the International Court are supposed to operate simply as legal authorities, without reference to their own cultural backgrounds, on the nuclear issue those from the nuclear-weapons states took a markedly less anti-nuclear stance than many from non-nuclear states. No judge took a line incompatible with the policy of his or her own government. International law, on its own without reference to any objective standard such as was afforded by a divinely authorized 'natural law', was unable to provide an independent criterion that could override the partial perceptions of individual member states. The only conceivable superior authority to which appeal could be made is the United Nations itself; and it is open to question whether this has, or even ought to have, the standing required to act as ultimate arbiter in the manner of the mediaeval church.

To the pacifist, in any case (and indeed to many others), reflection on the Just War tradition may seem something of an academic exercise. When has reflection on Just War principles ever prevented war from breaking out? What restraint have these principles ever exercised on the belligerents once the fighting gets desperate? Are they anything more than a means by which Christians have been able to salve their consciences when taking part in war, a compromise between a theoretically non-violent Christianity and the practical imperatives imposed by civic loyalties? And are they still in any sense adequate to the task of giving guidance to politicians and strategists when any use of force may rapidly escalate to unprecedented levels and when violent conflict is liable to break out, not between nation states with accountable governments, but between ethnic and even religious groups within the territory of a single country?

The pessimism implicit in these questions is understandable. But ultimately it is the same pessimism which may greet any attempt to lift or alleviate the curse of Cain, including the pacifist project itself. War, it can be argued, is endemic in the human race. Nations will fight each other until one or other is victorious, until both are exhausted, or unless a more powerful force is interposed between them. Apart from the undoubted success (in this respect) of the European Union, the only policy which can be shown historically to have prevented war has nothing to do with international institutions or peace movements but is the formation of alliances to maintain a balance of power. The evident folly of initiating war with massively destructive modern weapons cannot be relied upon to deter the ambitions of a ruthless aggressor. Once battle is engaged, no one can predict what atrocities the loser may commit to avoid total defeat. Even a religion such as Christianity, with its clear imperative to renounce violence, has again and again been an accomplice to warlike intentions. Against such powerful instincts and well-established military cultures, now made still more lethal by modern armaments, Just War theorizing and pacifist refusal to engage are alike 'academic'.

Only force, or the threat of it, is capable of saving the world from unprecedented catastrophe.

Our argument has been that this pessimism is no longer justified. The last half-century, with its new international institutions, with a new consensus on the inviolability of human rights, with an effective diminution of the freedom of sovereign states to initiate aggression and with a common agenda to conserve an increasingly fragile environment, has arguably given the world at least the promise of an international order that could greatly reduce the risk of major armed conflict. The question before us now is not so much whether the Just War tradition has ever prevented wars in the past and restrained the intentions of belligerents as whether it has a part to play in the contemporary striving of humanity to reduce the risks of war taking place and whether it can still provide moral and theological justification for the Christian non-pacifist position.

In a sense this amounts to casting it in a new role. Historically, it is unlikely that Just War theorists ever imagined that their reasoning would actually prevent wars taking place. In antiquity, in the Middle Ages, and indeed up to the First World War, the likelihood of war was taken for granted. Despite all the grievous suffering it might cause, war was assumed to be an option rulers might follow when other means of protecting their interests or gaining their objectives had failed; moreover its successful prosecution could lead to fame and honour beyond anything promised by the arts of peace. In these circumstances the theorists had little chance of influencing the course of events: they aspired rather to guide the conscience of Christian rulers contemplating war and of individual Christians who had to decide whether to take part in it. 'Thou shalt not kill' was a divine and universal prohibition; but the apparent necessity of war meant that there must be exemptions. Some classes of people, such as the clergy, could never be exempted.[9] But in time of war a Christian man could legitimately take up arms with the intention of killing an enemy so long as the Just War conditions were fulfilled – so long, that is, as the war was engaged in for the right reasons and waged in accordance with 'just' principles.

It is therefore unfair to criticize the Just War tradition for not having succeeded in preventing wars. Nor should it surprise us that the tradition has made only a minor contribution to the modern 'laws of war'. Though it does of course contain the principle of 'discrimination' (forbidding the deliberate killing of non-combatants), its emphasis and approach are somewhat different from that of recent Christian and humanitarian thinking. It is concerned, not with individual responsibility, but with strategic aims and tactical options. As its name implies, the criterion it invokes is 'justice'. If an aggressor has disturbed international order and committed a wrong that must be put right, the question is, in what circumstances can one be sure that the righting of the wrong will do more good than harm, and what tactical rules must be observed in order that the war may remain 'just' and not descend to a level of barbarism such that it should never have been engaged upon in the first place? These are questions for rulers and commanders, not subordinate officers and individual servicemen. Matters such as the safety of non-combatants or the treatment of prisoners receive little attention in a tradition derived, not from any humanitarian principles, but from a concept of justice that goes back to Stoic philosophy and beyond. Recent Christian thinking, by contrast, tends to start from a principle found in scripture as well as in natural law, namely the absolute inviolability of the innocent, which is necessarily a matter not just for the commander but for the individual. The Nuremberg trials in 1947 placed responsibility firmly on the individual to respect the difference between the legitimate (or 'just') killing of a combatant enemy and the killing (which is murder) of an unarmed civilian; and modern military manuals reflect the same principle. Moreover, the 'proportionality' which is such an important element in the Just War tradition, if defined as the avoidance of excessive casualties and destruction, is now seen to depend on the professionalism of servicemen as much as on the tactical decisions of generals. This shift of attention from politicians and generals to subordinate officers and individuals, and the apparent priority of the principle of the protection of the innocent at all costs over the abstract concept of justice, might make us think that the Just War tradition has lost some of its purchase on the realities of war and on the Christian conscience today.

Yet it is arguable that these considerations were always implicit in Just War thinking, even if they have become explicit in modern times. Certainly recent events have shown the tradition to be still very much alive. Not only has it played a significant part in the debate on the ethics of nuclear deterrence; its principles were widely invoked in the discussions leading up to the Gulf War in 1991. Admittedly there were doubtless other less academic factors which caused the opening of hostilities, ranging from concern for supplies of oil to the personal and political reputation of George Bush. But (at least in Britain) the issue was vigorously discussed in moral terms which respected the principles of Just War doctrine. It was argued that Iraq had invaded another sovereign state in defiance of the UN Charter and must be repelled ('just cause'); the objective of military action was to restore the integrity of frontiers and re-establish international authority ('right intention'); the operation had been formally authorized by the international community through a Security Council resolution ('lawful authority'); it had a 'reasonable prospect of success'; and the use of 'smart weapons', absolute superiority in the air and well deployed ground troops would ensure that the degree of force exerted on Iraq and the likely casualties would be 'in proportion' to the object to be achieved, namely the expulsion of Iraqi forces from Kuwait. These traditional Just War arguments persuaded many Christians that the Desert Storm campaign was not merely acceptable to their conscience but was a duty laid upon member states of the United Nations of which the Charter had been flouted; but it was the last category, that of 'proportionality', which caused most misgivings. In an age when the actual conduct of hostilities may be seen by millions on their TV screens and when it is impossible to conceal the scale of casualties suffered and inflicted, what level of death, wounding and destruction would be publicly acceptable as 'proportionate' to the objective? Might the massive exploitation of technological superiority in missiles and aircraft, even if it greatly reduced the risk of casualties to the allies, nevertheless cause injury and suffering to Iraqis (particularly civilians) 'disproportionate' to the scale of the military operation? In the event, despite the claims made for the limited damage caused by 'smart weapons', it was this question of proportion which caused most unease: and the ruthless bombing of retreating Iraqi troops on the Basra road, causing thousands of enemy casualties with little apparent military justification, forced many to the conclusion that the war had been 'unjust' in its conduct if not in its intention.

It is indeed the difficulty of applying the criterion of proportionality in modern conditions which most seriously calls into question claims by belligerents that the wars they wage are just.[10] In the European Christendom in which Aquinas developed the principles of the 'Just War', the practice of making proportionality-calculations must have been so familiar, so embedded in the culture, that in the discussion of the ethics of warfare it would have hardly merited special attention. For the whole of mediaeval trade and commerce was based on belief in the 'just price' for goods or services.

Prices were calculated by the intrinsic use-value of things, not simply by their exchange-value as determined by the market. Elusive as the concept of the 'just price' undoubtedly was, the habit of proportioning prices to use-value was endemic. The huge amount of effort made by theologians, bishops and preachers to stamp out avarice and extortion is proof of belief in the theoretical validity, as well as of the practical difficulty, of the proportionality, or 'just price', principle.

In trade, then, the proportionality principle was taken for granted. But today, in a world where prices are determined by exchange-values in the market, the very concept of proportionality becomes deeply problematic. Indeed under economic conditions of perfect competition the vice of avarice or the practice of extortion would become logical impossibilities, because these vices and their opposing virtues would have no place in the theoretical underpinnings of the system. However, as the existence of public disgust at the avarice of 'fat cats' shows, there is widespread disbelief in market forces as defenders of moral decency. The market cannot be trusted to deliver an ethically tolerable society. Mrs Thatcher notwithstanding, people want and demand that it be bucked.

Regulation of the activities of market forces, though demanded and necessary, remains problematic. And for precisely parallel reasons, the concept of proportionality has also become problematic for modern belligerents. In our post-Clausewitzian, market-dominated society belligerent behaviour is governed essentially by a market-system of morality, in which the principle of proportionality as a means of regulating war becomes all but unintelligible. In the sixteenth century the successes of rapacious adventurers in making disproportionate profits by stealing the lands and natural resources of the 'Indians' became scandalous to the conservative Dominican moralists of Salamanca, who began

to recognize that people had inalienable *legal* rights simply
because they were human. Today determining the just price
for military operations – say in calculating the just level of
casualties to be inflicted or suffered in a particular engagement – has to be conducted in the absence of any objective
principle or criterion. It may be a matter simply of what
public opinion will tolerate or what the professionals believe
to be appropriate. There is no culture of 'just prices' for
victory in modern post-Clausewitzian warfare. And, in the
present climate of moral relativism, there is no consensus
on how to create one.[11]

A second Just War principle which has become difficult
to apply is that of 'discrimination'. This principle can be
stated thus: there is simply no purpose, however noble, for
the attainment of which it is licit, as a means to an end,
intentionally to kill, or to consent (even conditionally) to
the killing of, people who are innocent of doing or threatening to do us any harm.

This principle should apply both in the waging and in the
deterrence of war; but it is not universally accepted. There is,
for example, the objection put forward by Michael Walzer in
his discussion of siege warfare and the immunity from attack
of innocent civilians in the besieged city. He argues that
civilian citizens who, having been given the chance to leave
the city by the besieging forces, choose for whatever reason
to remain, thereby lose their normal immunity from direct
attack. This is so even though their 'choice' may well have
been made under extreme duress by the defending commander who wants civilians in his city as a kind of protective
shield, or to help him in other ways.[12] Walzer's argument
is founded (a) on the fact that sieges are permitted by the
laws of war, and (b) that without the above-mentioned reser-
vation concerning civilian immunity sieges may well turn
out to be impossible. Yet Walzer is open to the criticism
that, despite their choice to stay, these civilians still fail to

constitute any kind of threat to the besieging forces.[13] And if they are no threat, how come they have lost their immunity from attack and have now become legitimate military targets? For even if they are in the city 'voluntarily' they are still not combatants, and surely ought to be allowed the immunity normally granted in Just War theory to those innocent of doing, or threatening to do, any harm to their opponents? *Mutatis mutandis* the same argument can be made about the immunity from direct attack of civilians in a city under aerial bombardment, or even of those caught up in guerrilla warfare.

Now Walzer may reply that the civilians' *choice* to stay despite being given the chance to leave must make *some* difference to the question of moral responsibility. But what the argument shows is at most that things are not quite as clear cut as the discrimination principle at first suggests.[14] Even if the responsibility falling on the various players for the deaths of the civilians in a siege cannot always be clearly identified, this does not alter the essential principle of the inviolability of the innocent in war. The principle of discrimination retains its absolute validity.

But can this principle still be applied? In modern war, are there any 'innocents'? The twentieth-century concept of 'total war' implies that almost any section of the civilian population may be involved in 'the war effort', and so cease to be strictly non-combatants with immunity from attack. Certainly the very large number of civilian casualties in recent wars suggests that the principle of non-combatant immunity is no longer thought to apply (unless it is being ruthlessly disregarded). The 'collateral damage' consequent upon the use of modern conventional bombardments – let alone nuclear or biological weapons – is now accepted by strategists as a regrettable but necessary feature of war. If virtually the whole population is regarded as committed to the struggle, their exposure to attack, even if to be avoided so far as possible, is nevertheless regarded as legitimate. In this case the principle of discrimination appears to have become obsolete. Yet there is a way of defining 'innocent' which may give it at least some sphere of application. It can be asked of any section in the population – such as farmers, housewives, children or the elderly – however much they hate the enemy and are in solidarity with others in the struggle against him: Do they in any sense constitute a threat to the success of his military activities? If not, then they surely count as 'innocent', and the principle of discrimination should continue to have at least this limited application.[15]

Further problems arise when we consider the principle of 'just cause'. From Aquinas onwards, the tradition is quite clear that a Just War may be waged only for the righting of a clearly-defined wrong that has been committed. This implies that the objective of a war must always be strictly limited, a point which might seem to be endorsed by Clausewitz's principle that war is simply a particular means of pursuing a specified objective (though in Clausewitz's thinking it is in fact cancelled out by his insistence that one may proceed as far as the total annihilation of one's opponent). But is a limited war any longer possible in view of modern technologies, the globalization of economic power and the widespread disintegration of unstable states? May the Falklands War have been the last example of a war with the aim of simply righting a specified wrong? And what of irregular wars (by far the commonest sort now and in the foreseeable future) which are nearly always conducted for some absolute principle rather than for the righting of a specific injustice and are seldom brought to an end by the achievement of some limited objective? It is true that from the point of view of the international community such wars may look less like wars than disturbance of the peace by groups of organized criminals; in which case the appropriate armed response is more like a police action than a war, with the limited objective of restoring order in the region. To this extent it may be called 'just'. But the international character of the operation itself raises a further problem.

This problem relates to 'just intention' and may be illustrated by the Gulf War of 1991. Was it not designed, *pace* Bush's rhetoric about establishing a new world order, simply to eject Saddam from Kuwait in accordance with the UN Charter? Not everyone agrees that this was the real aim. There are British Muslims, claiming to speak for a majority of their co-religionists the world over, who insist that the true purpose of the war was to maintain oil supplies to the West, to keep the Islamic world divided, and to perpetuate Western dominance over the Arabs.[16] The question here is not whether or not such plausible claims are warranted, but whether in such a case the concept of *recta intentio* any longer has application. In mediaeval or renaissance or even Napoleonic times the aim of a war was whatever purpose the sovereign belligerent had in waging it. Its aim was *his* aim, for which he was answerable. In those circumstances there was sense in insisting that, to be just, the sovereign belligerent's aim (his *intentio*) must be right (*recta*): namely to establish peace.[17] But can a huge unwieldy assemblage of variegated states, armies, economies and interests such as was required for dealing with the Kuwait crisis be said to have any clear aim or *intentio* at all, let alone a right one? Who was in a position to say authoritatively what the aim was?

Of course one answer to this question was that the aim of the war was the aim set by the United Nations through resolutions of the Security Council. But the United Nations is not a sovereign state, and was not itself a belligerent actor in the war against Saddam. The coalition which waged the war under the aegis of the United Nations (Charter, Article 51) was a coalition of belligerents; but the United Nations was not itself a belligerent. Of course, one can speak of the Security Council's aim, and judge that it was *recta*. But this was not necessarily the same thing as the aim of the belligerents who joined in the coalition, who may have been motivated by a variety of interests. It may be granted that the Security Council had a right intention in lending its authority to the war. This intention was embodied in resolutions, and certainly did not extend further than removing Saddam from Kuwait (hence the decision not to pursue the war after that objective had been achieved). But here we are trespassing on the territory of lawful authority rather than of *recta intentio* as Just War theory envisages it, for in international relations theory only states, because they are sovereign actors on the international stage, can be regarded as responsible for war-aims, just as the sovereign prince of old was. It thus made sense to speak of (say) Argentina's aim in occupying the Falkland Islands, or Indonesia's aim of invading East Timor, or Saddam's aim in annexing Kuwait. But these aims are not on a par with the aim of the Security Council in authorizing belligerent action. And it is quite another thing to speak of a coherent *intentio* among a coalition of interests cobbled together to fight a war under its authority.

It has to be admitted that here we are venturing on to new, tricky ground. The fact is that the United Nations is neither a sovereign actor nor a government with full authority over other actors. It is a bastard creature of the twentieth-century's history. Had it been a sovereign belligerent in the Kuwait war, it would have been both judge and jury in its own cause – the Machiavellian anomaly in international relations that the United Nations itself was set up to overcome. On the other hand, had it been a sovereign government, it would have had its own forces to deploy – as Boutros Boutros Ghali recommended in his *Agenda for Peace*. Unfortunately, it was neither, and had to cope as best it could under the far from unambiguous terms of the Charter. The fact is that the United Nations is, and was intended to be, in hock to the 'great powers', that is the major sovereign states who won the Second World War. But things have changed so radically since 1945 that this founding principle is no longer enough. True, a readjustment took place when the Republic of China replaced Taiwan; but this did not alter the underlying principle of the dominance of the 'great powers'. The problem today is that power has been radically redistributed in the world while the United Nations has been unable to accommodate fully to this fact. It is neither a global sovereign authority nor simply a forum for building peace and security among states without recourse to violence. Its ambivalence is an expression of a world in drastic transition, struggling to be reborn. It is this ambivalence which raises unavoidably the question of the applicability, in modern circumstances, of Just War principles, including in particular that of 'right intention' in the use of military force for the settlement of disputes.

There is a further feature of the modern world which may be thought to make Just War reasoning problematic. The tradition was premised upon war being waged between states (or 'princes') for the purpose of righting the wrong which one of them had committed. Its application today (as in the case of the Gulf War of 1991) similarly presupposes that some act of aggression has taken place which it is necessary ('just') to repel and punish. But the end of the twentieth century has seen a significant amount of warfare conducted, not between states, but within states. The question then is not so much whether a neighbouring state or alliance should go to war with an aggressor as whether the international community should intervene within the boundaries of a state and exercise force to prevent genocide, 'ethnic cleansing' or some other major violation of human rights. The dilemma this presents can be expressed in terms of two apparently incompatible Articles of the UN Charter. On the one hand there is an absolute veto on any use of military force to intervene in the domestic affairs of another state (Article 2.7). On the other hand the member states are obliged (Articles 55, 56) to protect and promote human rights to the best of their ability, and recent events (as in Somalia, in Algeria, in former Yugoslavia) show that this may not be possible without the use of force. Can the Just War tradition help to decide whether such action should be taken? Or (to put the question concisely) is there such a thing as 'just intervention'?

Some traditional principles certainly seem relevant. One that is regularly appealed to is that of 'lawful authority'. Before considering intervention the international community is keen to be assured that military action is authorized by the UN through the Security Council and is legal according to international law – and it is arguable that (were this practicable) the UN Charter should be amended in order to remove the apparent illegality of intervention in the affairs of an autonomous state in such circumstances.[18] 'Just cause', again, seems well provided for by the moral necessity of protecting the innocent from deliberate attack. But 'right intention' is particularly difficult to assess. A major part of the problem of military intervention is the lack of a clear objective. If force must be used to protect one part of the population, what then? Can this foreign force remain neutral if the oppressed mount a counter-attack? Is the object to create a 'safe haven', to introduce a long-term peace-keeping force, or to vacate the field as soon as possible? Uncertainty about the future role (or 'intention') of the intervening force is a major cause of hesitation. 'Just proportion', again, is singularly difficult to apply. What level of casualties, if any, will the intervening countries and their public opinion tolerate for their own troops? What degree of force is it appropriate to use in response to the alleged violation of human rights? There seems no precedent for answering these questions, and in practice the issue is likely to be debated less in Just War terms than as a matter of balancing the strength of the humanitarian concern voiced by the international community against the practical difficulties and long-term implications of military actions.[19] Only a few of the traditional Just War arguments seem to gain any purchase on these increasingly prevalent threats to peace. In this respect, again, many may believe that the tradition is obsolete.

This discussion has shown that there are serious difficulties in applying Just War principles with any stringency to modern armed conflicts, even though they have been explicitly appealed to in connection with some recent military engagements. But it is this tradition which for many centuries furnished the Christian conscience with justification for disregarding the apparently pacifist mandate of the gospel and for engaging in warfare. If this justification can no longer be maintained, it might seem to follow that Christians today, if they are to remain faithful to the teaching of Christ, have no option but the pacifist one, and that their churches should publicly refuse to endorse the threat or use of force in international affairs. But before drawing this conclusion it is important to bear in mind another strand of Christian thinking which, though implicit in the Just War tradition, appeals not to the philosophical concept of 'justice' but to the principle, explicitly stated in the Bible, of the inviolability of innocent life. It is this principle, now widely accepted, which has given us the 'laws of war' protecting the sick, the injured and prisoners of war and imposing on belligerents the duty to avoid targeting non-combatants; which has sustained the fundamental objection to a policy of nuclear deterrence (that it acquiesces in the probable slaughter of large numbers of civilians and the maiming of many more still unborn); which adds moral pressure to technical military reasons for developing ever more accurate (or 'smart') weapons so as to reduce what is euphemistically called 'collateral damage' (which usually means civilian casualties) to a minimum; and which is the criterion many people will instinctively use today when considering whether a given military operation, apparently required for the protection of human rights or the re-establishment of international order, is compatible with the Christian conscience.

In point of fact it may be argued that certain elements of the Just War tradition (particularly 'just cause' and 'lawful authority'), along with the religious and humanitarian consensus that the innocent must be protected, are embodied in the UN Charter, and that this now provides a guide to the Christian conscience which replaces both. Article 52 limits the permissible pretexts for war to self-defence in case of attack by an aggressor, and then only until the international community has been able to mediate; Article 42 authorizes the UN to use force if necessary to cause the aggressor to desist; and Articles 55 and 56 (in uneasy tension with the foregoing) lay the duty on member states to protect the human rights of individuals, with the implication that in serious cases of genocide or 'ethnic cleansing' it might be necessary to intervene by force. On the basis of these provisions there is an emerging international consensus that:

(1) no use or threat of force is permissible that is not in accordance with the UN Charter;
(2) military action should normally be engaged upon only with the authority of a UN Security Council Resolution;
(3) it must be conducted with the minimum force required to achieve the objective and with the utmost practicable protection of non-combatants;
(4) all personnel must adhere strictly to internationally agreed laws of war and rules of engagement.

The consensus undoubtedly represents a significant advance in humanity's striving for peace and order and deserves the widest possible endorsement, including that of Christians. Indeed it was concern whether the Nato campaign in the Balkans in 1999 strictly observed these conditions that underlay much of the anxious questioning to which that campaign was subjected. In particular, the duty to support the United Nations and its agencies and to adhere scrupulously to the Charter is laid upon all who are committed to work for peace. This does not mean, of course, that the UN is above reproach or can claim ultimate authority over the conscience of individuals. Security Council or General Assembly resolutions represent only the views of the majority that voted for them, and may well have been influenced by the political interests of the most powerful states. Yet the degree to which they take account of the traditional principles of just cause, right intention and lawful authority before authorizing military operations, and insist on the protection of the innocent in their conduct, arguably provides a criterion by which Christians may decide whether they can in conscience approve them and take part in them. On the other hand, our discussion has suggested that the difficulty and uncertainty involved in applying this criterion may drive more and more Christians to consider seriously adopting a pacifist stance. But before we discuss this further, there is another option to be considered.

5

Non-Violence and the Pacifist Alternative

The sharp alternative traditionally presented between pacifism and non-pacifism, bearing arms and refusing military service, involvement in conflict and resolute standing aside from it, has been blurred in recent years by the emergence of a new concept, that of 'non-violent action' on a massive scale. A succession of profound political changes has taken place in this century as a result neither of free democratic action nor of the use of force but of the determined will of a large section of the population expressed in various forms of 'passive resistance' or 'non-violent action'. The stories of Gandhi or of Martin Luther King, of the 'velvet revolution' in East Europe in 1989, of the ending of apartheid in South Africa, or of the peaceful overthrow of dictatorships in the Philippines and Indonesia in the 1980s and 1990s, represent a significant trend in the history of revolutions: men and women have become aware of the power which may be wielded by sheer force of numbers and strength of will, without recourse to weapons of any kind, against even the most ruthless and well-organized dictatorships. This experience (in terms of world history) is relatively new. Does it mean that there has now opened up some common ground between pacifists and non-pacifists? Is 'non-violence' a form of action sufficiently effective to satisfy

Christians who hold responsibility for justice and order but sufficiently bloodless to be conscientiously engaged in by convinced pacifists? Has the twentieth century, despite being the most violent century in history, produced a new resolution of the age-old tension between these two ways of interpreting the Christian faith?

Certainly there has been an impressive series of recent denominational and ecumenical statements to the effect that this may now be the case. A typical instance is in the Pastoral Letter of the Roman Catholic Bishops of the United States, *The Challenge of Peace: God's Promise and our Response* (1983). This contains the optimistic statement:

> Non-violent resistance offers a common ground of agreement for those individuals who choose the option of Christian pacifism ... and those who choose the option of lethal force allowed by the theology of the just war.[1]

This sentiment is echoed in ecumenical documents, which regularly speak of non-violence as an 'active dynamic and a constructive force',[2] of a 'culture of active non-violence' and of the development of 'civilian-based defence';[3] and such statements are regularly followed by demands that this new option should urgently receive the theological appraisal and practical testing which it deserves. It is evident that a large body of reflective and influential Christians has come to see 'non-violence' as the key to effective Christian witness in the conflicts which beset the world today and as an enterprise in which the pacifist and non-pacifist traditions of Christianity may at last be united. Is this optimism justified?

Before trying to answer this question it is necessary for us to clarify some of the terms being used. 'Violence' is a word which most people assume they understand: the difference between being persuaded into a course of action by words or gestures and being forced into it by 'violence' seems clear enough. When the European Convention on Compensation of Victims of Violent Crimes (1983) was drafted, it was not felt necessary to define 'violent': it was assumed that everyone would know the difference between, say, a felony committed when no one was around and one which involved physical attack on a victim – the fact that the criminal might have used 'violence' to break open a window was rightly seen as irrelevant. Violent crime is understood without difficulty as crime involving physical injury for the person or persons criminally attacked. And the same might be thought to apply to collective actions by crowds, political parties or interest groups: so long as no physical hurt is caused intentionally they would not normally be called 'violent'. But now theologians, as well as philosophers, are tending to find the matter much less simple. It became a commonplace proposition of Liberation Theology in the 1960s and 1970s that there is such a thing as 'structural violence', that is to say, even if no physical violence is being exerted on a person there may be forces in the structures of society which effectively limit the freedom of that person, which are equivalent to forms of oppression which use physical violence and which may therefore be called 'violent'.

There was of course nothing new about using the word 'violence' metaphorically: one can speak of an insult 'doing violence' to one's self-esteem without fear of being misunderstood – no one will think that one suffered a literal slap on the face. But 'structural violence' was more than this. It was a phrase deliberately used to alert people to the malign influence of social factors of which the majority are unaware. An economic system which rewards the wealthy and leaves the poor destitute is easy enough to criticize; but given the difficulties involved in changing it and the apparently inexorable economic forces which tend to reinforce it the instinct of most people is to assume that it must be accepted for the time being, in the hope that perhaps gradual modifications of the system may eventually produce a fairer distribution of the country's resources. The effect of introducing the word 'violence' in this context is to challenge the assumption that the situation can be allowed to continue indefinitely. If there is a sense in which it is actually inflicting violence on a whole section of the population then it is clearly unacceptable to Christian opinion. 'Structural violence' is by definition a state of affairs which needs to be brought to an end for simple reasons of humanity and equity. But the phrase is also one which introduces an element of ambiguity into the language. 'Violence' is not being used metaphorically: tangible consequences of the social structures are being indicated. But equally it is not being used in the usual sense of physical assault, since these consequences may be such things as endemic poverty or the lack of any political voice.

Since then, similar ambiguities have begun to appear in other contexts. It might be thought, for example, that there was a clear distinction between physical (or 'violent') torture and psychological torture; but *all* torture is now commonly called 'violent'. Similarly, the distinction is fairly obvious between active hostilities and the imposition of sanctions; but it is not uncommon to hear of sanctions being described – understandably in view of the suffering they cause, usually to those least able to influence policy – as an act of violence. It is no surprise therefore to find that the World Council of Churches' 'Programme to Overcome Violence' is concerned with far more than physical violence. It deliberately seeks to extend the concept to areas of social justice and personal relationships: 'Unjust political and economic institutions, racism, sexism all create violence.'[4] This, of course, is perfectly legitimate so far as the use of language is concerned. Just as 'peace' is recognized to imply far more than the absence of conflict, with the consequence that its range of meaning is greatly enlarged, so 'violence', or at least the potential for violence, can be detected in a wide range of human behaviour and organization which might otherwise be passed over as harmless. This is, after all, precisely the way in which Jesus taught. By bracketing anger and insult with homicide he drew attention to the possible moral seriousness of acts and words normally regarded as trivial or harmless.[5] Similarly, to call behaviour 'violent' which normally escapes censure (being within the law) is to bring it within the sphere of serious moral judgment. But at the same time it is important not to let this enlargement of the concept blur distinctions which are essential for other purposes. Housebreaking is not the same as violent crime, racist language is not the same as violent assault on racist grounds. We need to be alert to the confusions which may be caused by this somewhat imprecise extension of ordinary usage.

Another source of possible confusion is the word 'conflict'. 'The avoidance of conflict' is often stated to be the purpose of long-term peace initiatives. From the context we may be able to infer that what is meant is *violent* conflict; for conflict itself is inherent in the human condition and is not necessarily harmful, indeed may be actually enriching. People will have conflicting opinions, conflicting loyalties, conflicting interests; and the conflicts to which these give rise are the very stuff of social, political and even religious life. What matters is how these conflicts are managed. In the case of children, or of uncivilized societies, they may rapidly lead to blows; by contrast, one of the most obvious fruits of education and civilized experience is that conflicts are resolved, or at least peacefully lived with, without recourse to force by one side or the other. Some indeed might say that conflict at this level is not only inevitable but is a necessary part of being human: it is a mark of that curiosity, that will to excel and that passion for the truth which lie at the heart of civilized endeavour. It becomes damaging only when it can no longer be resolved by argument, persuasion or compromise and erupts into violence. To this extent it is misleading to speak of peacemaking and peacekeeping as 'the avoidance of conflict'. It is only *violent* conflict which must be avoided.

This leads us directly into the paradox created by talk of 'non-violent action'. Such action may be assumed to be a response to a serious conflict of interests; and, as we have just seen, the essence of the civilized arts is to resolve or contain conflict in such a way that none of the parties involved is tempted to resort to violence. In a liberal society, all action in pursuit of personal or group interests is by definition 'non-violent': if violence does break out, it must be restrained by the forces of law and order and the perpetrators duly punished. The problem arises, of course, when a society is not, in this sense, 'liberal', that is, when disproportionate power rests in the hands of a minority to the detriment of the majority, and people have no political or legal means of getting their legitimate grievances redressed. Such situations may lead, and have often led, to violent revolution; but recent experience has shown that there may be an alternative. Whether because the revolutionaries are too weakly armed, or because they have a genuine revulsion against using force, they may renounce the traditional form of armed uprising and opt for what is now called 'non-violent action', that is, the obtaining of their political ends by using various forms of pressure that stop short of actual violence. These have been successful on some notable occasions. Even when they fail, it can be claimed that less suffering is caused than in the often predictable failure of an armed rebellion.

What forms of pressure are these? In a democracy, the ultimate form of pressure is the ballot box: representatives who do not carry out the will of the electorate may lose their seats in the elected assembly. But between elections a democratically elected government may adopt policies that are deeply unpopular or even unjust, and pressure may legitimately be exerted on it through the media, through demonstrations on the streets, through lobbying of individual politicians or through 'industrial action' (by legal or illegal strikes). All of these are 'non-violent'; but none of them is what is normally meant today by 'non-violent action', which tends to involve much larger numbers of people and to take the form of a general strike, massive non-co-operation with the authorities, sit-down obstruction of means of transport and so forth. In principle these should result in no damage to persons or property (and therefore be strictly 'non-violent'). But in practice the line is easily crossed into activity that is, to some degree, violent and dangerous. Protesters against nuclear weapons installations, for example, though strictly unarmed and with allegedly peaceful intentions, may nevertheless damage property by gaining illegal entry. Protesters against the building of a by-pass may commit trespass on the contractors' site or disobey the orders of the police in a way which leaves the authorities with no option but to use a measure of violence for their physical removal. Such action often involves conflict with the law, and indeed those who take part in it may consciously break the law and accept the risk of punishment, often with actual gratitude for the publicity which it gives to their cause and for the opportunity of challenging the justice of the laws under which they are charged. But once they are involved in damage to property or breaking the law their non-violent action involves at least the risk of suffering violence to their own persons and unintentionally inflicting it on others.

These instances are sufficient for drawing attention to some of the ambiguities involved in any form of 'non-violent' action. In countries which enjoy a reasonable degree of political freedom and the protection of personal rights and liberties afforded by democratic government, these ambiguities seem to many people to make such action an unnecessary and often undesirable alternative to legitimate political action. But where there is a totalitarian regime, exerting severe economic and political oppression, the option is a serious one: the experience of the last few decades has opened up the possibility of effective change through organized passive resistance and non-co-operation that can render powerless the organs of state. In this context, 'non-violent action', which ranges from vigils and marches on the one hand to highly organized civic non-co-operation, sit-ins and hunger strikes on the other,[6] has been shown on numerous occasions to be a genuine and effective alternative to armed resistance and violent revolution. As Pope John Paul II observed in 1993:

> It seemed that the European order resulting from the Second World War ... could only be overturned by another war. Instead, it has been overcome by the non-violent commitment of people who, while refusing to yield to the force of power, succeeded time after time in finding effective ways of bearing witness to the truth.[7]

Nor are movements of this kind engaged in only by those who reject the use of violence on principle: the non-violent revolutions of the last twenty years have involved large numbers of people who were by no means committed to total non-violence but who deliberately opted for non-violent techniques to achieve their ends. Indeed it was on the basis of a popular consensus that non-violent means are preferable to the use of armed force that it was possible in Lithuania, Latvia and Estonia to include civilian-based defence in plans for protection against Soviet attack in 1991; and other countries, particularly Sweden, are now working seriously on incorporating a 'non-military resistance component' in their total defence policies.[8] To this extent such action may be judged to have bridged the divide between those who hold a pacifist position and those who are prepared to contemplate the use of force, at least as a last resort, in the tradition of the 'Just War'.

It is important not to overstate the case. Those who take part in non-violent action are not necessarily opposed to the use of force if their action fails: violence remains for many of them a legitimate option of last, or maybe only nearly-last, resort. Moreover non-violence is not a panacea: certain conditions have to be in place for it to have any hope of success. It is often remarked that Gandhi's policy of *satyagraha* was possible only because British rule in India was characterized by a scrupulous respect for the law – a more ruthless colonial power would have crushed the movement without difficulty. Similarly the East European revolutions of 1989 were favoured by movements within the entire Soviet empire which undermined the authority of government and created a high degree of sympathy among the police and the military for the non-violent protesters. Students of these movements agree that a number of practical considerations will bear on the question whether any particular project of non-violent liberation or political change is likely to be successful; and there can never be any guarantee that what began with non-violence may not end in violence. It is significant that amid a long line of ecumenical assemblies devoted to questions of justice, liberation and peaceful change and calling for urgent study of non-violent policies and techniques, two WCC conferences held in Northern Ireland (in 1983 and 1994) failed to make any specific recommendations for the development of non-violent action, and drew attention instead to 'the complexity of the international situation today and the actual experience of people regarding the use of violence for political ends'.[9] Similarly, the board of the Commission of the Churches on

International Affairs meeting in Zambia in 1994, though
seeking to promote peace with justice through conventional
methods of conflict resolution such as mediation, said nothing about non-violence as a genuine alternative to violence.[10]
These meetings were clearly having to face the reality of the
threat of violence posed by terrorist, para-military or tribal
movements, against which non-violent action may be
powerless. Valid and inspiring though the call to non-
violence may be in certain circumstances, in others it may
prove to be a dangerous form of rhetoric. In the present
state of the world, and indeed in the foreseeable future, it
is clearly premature to claim that it is the long awaited
resolution of pacifist and non-pacifist principles in Christianity. In 1987 the episcopal diocese of Washington, though
recognizing that non-violent resistance had been successfully used as a means to achieve human and civil rights
in the United States during the 1960s, confessed that they
were 'honestly troubled . . . by the claim that non-violent
resistance can be effective in settling conflicts between
nations'.[11]

Yet the non-violent option is not to be lightly dismissed.
Its successes have perhaps not yet received the attention they
deserve: being popular movements of (usually) anonymous
people they have not attracted the interest of academic his-
torians, and it may be that the traditional presumption of
Christian thought that force may be used, at least in the
last resort, in the interests of justice and peace has made
Christians less alert than they should be to the possibilities
of achieving the same objectives by non-violent action. There
is now a growing literature on the subject;[12] and the insistent
demands in ecumenical statements that it should receive
urgent study should not be dismissed simply on the grounds
that it does not always work. Even if its success up to the
present day has been more patchy than its advocates admit,
who knows what would happen if more public resources

were invested in training and disciplined preparation? There has, after all, been a significant shift in recent years in the role, and therefore the training, of professional armies, which are not being maintained primarily to wage national wars of self-defence (let alone of offence), but to prevent or intervene in wars between, or more often within, other nations. For this purpose they may be required to serve under international command and to use their weapons (like police) only in the last resort. This implies new models of military training and represents a notable advance in civilization's struggle towards peace. Moreover it points the way towards the training of unarmed civilian peacekeepers and the teaching of the skills needed to defeat despotic power without bloodshed. These are signs that non-violent action is becoming an increasingly realistic option, and one which surely holds great attraction for Christians. For is there not something at the very heart of Christianity which is incompatible with violence in any form? Whether one thinks of the teaching of Jesus to love one's enemies and to offer no resistance to evil, or of the doctrinal emphasis of Christianity on the willing acceptance of suffering and the redemptive power of altruistic self-sacrifice, any recourse to violence and armed force to achieve personal or political ends must seem like utter faithlessness to the Christian calling.

But is the church ready to adopt this option? The fact is that throughout its history the church has seldom protested against war as such: characteristically, and despite persistent minority protests, it has shown a degree of complicity in the warlike ambitions of rulers which seems to belie any serious faith in the possibility of eliminating the curse of Cain in this or any generation. Reflection on the Crusades or the Wars of Religion, or even just a walk round the monuments to military men in Westminster Abbey, shows how deeply the church has been implicated in the pursuit of political and even religious objectives by force of arms. Could it now dissociate itself completely from the disciplined use of force in the interests of international order or territorial integrity? Moreover is there not military imagery embedded in Christian spirituality – the sword of truth, the breastplate of salvation, the 'good fight' that must be waged against the powers of darkness? Has not the sacrifice of Christ provided a pattern and inspiration for young warriors prepared to die for their country? Is there not a case to be made out for the virtues cultivated in the armed forces – loyalty, self-sacrifice, obedience, alertness to the needs of others – being a profound preparation for the conduct required by the Christian life? Can we never believe that God is on the side of our armies, however just our cause? Can no Christian soldier ever pray for victory? In short, is it conceivable that the church could dissociate itself entirely from war and declare that violence is not an option for Christians?

Surprisingly, this question might receive an answer slightly different today from that which would have been given even twenty years ago. In the two world wars of this century, as in countless previous European wars, the God of the Christians was shamelessly invoked to protect and prosper the armies on both sides of the conflict and victory was celebrated with full religious ritual. Yet, before the end of the second, influential Christian voices were being raised questioning not only the conduct of the war against Hitler but its ultimate objective. Bishop George Bell of Chichester not merely protested (on traditional 'Just War' grounds) against the indiscriminate bombing of cities but pleaded for a recognition of those humane and non-belligerent elements in German society whose existence justified early negotiation for peace. Forty years later, the recapture of the Falkland Islands by British Forces was celebrated in St Paul's Cathedral, not by a victory service, but by a commemoration which stressed the human cost to both sides of the conflict and the urgency of reconciliation. Similarly, the fortieth and fiftieth anniversaries of turning points in the Second World War were commemorated by church services expressing penitence for past belligerence and commitment to efforts for peace rather than any sprit of triumphalism. Meanwhile papal statements, after a long period of condoning Christian participation in rebellion against tyranny[13] or wars for national defence (reaffirmed in 1956 by Pius XII[14]), have moved forward to John Paul II's condemnation of *all* war as a 'totally unacceptable' means of settling international disputes.[15] In short, there has been a discernible shift in the public posture of the churches from their historic identification with the fortunes of the armed forces of their country towards a penitential recognition of the inevitable evils of war and a determination to bring all possible resources of mediation and reconciliation to the task of preventing its recurrence.

This shift seems likely to continue; and as it does so it may well foster an enhanced Christian commitment to promotion of arms control and confidence building, to education in peace studies, to humanitarian and development aid towards eradicating the long-term courses of war, to training in conflict resolution, to support for the United Nations and the rule of international law and to the promotion of peace by all available means. It may even impel Christians to recognize that the centuries-old involvement of the church in warfare has been a form of apostasy from its faith in the non-violent redemption wrought by Christ. But it is also overwhelmingly probable that, at least in the near future, the world will continue to see gross violations of human rights, instances of territorial aggression and 'ethnic cleansing', and outrageous disparities of wealth and resources which contain the seeds of violent conflict. In the face of these threats the majority of Christians have instinctively aligned themselves with the great majority of their fellow citizens in relying upon the force of arms, even if

only in the last resort, to restore order, to save innocent lives
from violence and oppression and to provide an ultimate
sanction against those who would otherwise threaten
international peace and order. Even if a growing number
of church leaders and an increasing segment of church
members now tend towards a more explicitly pacifist stance
(a tendency towards which the witness of pacifists will have
made a significant contribution), the silent majority in the
pews will need much persuading not to acquiesce in the use
of force as a last resort and in accordance with some form
of the principles of the Just War. But it is precisely for
this purpose of persuasion that the pacifist tradition is so
important today. Indeed, it can be argued that the time may
be ripe for church leaders to initiate a broader debate on
this issue, a debate which might eventually lead to pacifism
becoming the norm for the churches instead of a minority
movement within them.

In the past, pacifism was seen, not as an option for whole
churches, but as a vocation to be lived out either by individuals or by relatively small associations of Christians such
as the Religious Society of Friends or the Anglican Pacifist
Fellowship. This was not seen as a withdrawal from the
realities of violent conflict or from the tensions and ambiguities entailed in the resolute following of Christian principles
in the complex world of today. As Roger Wilson, a Quaker
pacifist, has written when reflecting on the war against
Hitler, 'I had a far deeper sense of spiritual unity with those
of my friends in the fighting services who, detesting war as
deeply as I did, yet felt that there was no other way in which
they could share the agony of the world, than I had with
those pacifists who talked as if the sufferings of the world
could be turned off like a water tap if only politicians would
talk sensibly together.'[16] It is simply not true that pacifism
entails a refusal to share the sufferings of humanity or to
bear the cost of creating peace. Not only have pacifists given

impressive testimony of their courage and solidarity with others through ambulance service, humanitarian work and costly mediation efforts: their problems of conscience and moral dilemmas are no less agonizing than for other Christians. These are well illustrated by the following paragraphs of a paper privately circulated by Peter Jarman, an active pacifist:

Two years ago I went with a serving British army officer to help train paramilitary troops in peacekeeping operations within a disputed territory of Southern Russia after a civil war there. As we were about to board our return flight to Moscow, he asked, 'I really appreciated working with a Quaker pacifist. Tell me, what do you think about the NATO bombing of the Bosnian Serbs?' 'In all honesty,' I replied, 'I cannot criticize those who ordered that bombing, but I would not have pressed the bomb release.' 'If you will not criticize that action, then in all honesty you should have been prepared to release those bombs,' the officer insisted. 'Your vocation is to be a soldier, and I appreciate the predicaments that this vocation places you in. However, my vocation is that of a pacifist peacebuilder,' I replied . . .

In the hard days of Soviet Communism in 1982, I met with considerable difficulty a member of the informal group of 'dissidents' in Moscow established to build up trust between the Soviet Union and the United States. As we emerged from a metro station opposite a giant statue of Lenin, he asked, 'I have always wanted to meet a Quaker. Tell me, what would Quakers do with a Hitler or a Stalin?' After giving a talk about pacifism three years before this to a group of young Communists in Leningrad, I was asked by one of them, 'What would you do if you were a black in South Africa or a Russian after the invasion of the Nazis?' To these questions I answered, 'I don't know. All I can say is that I hope to help create a society in which Hitlers and Stalins cannot assume power...'

Would I myself not use violence in any circumstance? If I saw my wife or children being attacked would I not instinctively seek to prevent this, using force if necessary? I have never been placed in such a position and I do not know what I would do. If I used violence to protect my own family, why, ask military people, would I not be prepared to use violence to protect other families of my kindred and kin? This is the perennial pacifist predicament.

In travelling into disputed territories in the former Soviet Union I have been guarded by armed soldiers. I was unarmed but was making a pragmatic compromise with idealistic pacifism for without such a guard governments were not prepared to let me travel into those territories and I needed to do that in order to meet the people there, to see the destruction of property and to get to the other side.

So, yes, I am a pragmatist and a compromiser, I admit, and I am left with prickings of conscience and unresolved dilemmas.

But 'unresolved dilemmas' need not inhibit positive action. As another pacifist, Tony Kempster, has written, 'To sit and wait for war so that one can be a conscientious objector is an untenable position because we are part of society and experience the benefits and deficits like everyone else. To achieve real change it is often necessary to compromise and assist in developments which are steps towards the overall aim. We must always reach for the possible as it shows itself.' A pacifist is constantly on the look-out for means of mitigating the underlying causes of conflict and for managing conflict non-violently. Peter Jarman offers the following examples:

> During the 1920s, the Quakers and others persevered in seeking to persuade the British and French governments to ameliorate the vindictive effects of the Versailles peace treaty upon the German peoples. For they saw in this act of revenge and humiliation of these peoples the seed of another war. This concern gave effect to living that life that takes away the occasion of war – to engage in conflict mitigation at an early stage before the peat of people's self respect and security begins to smoulder and catch fire fuelled by the vitriolic rhetoric of dictators like Hitler.

> When violence erupts, an unarmed pacifist may be able to travel between the warring parties as Quakers did for example during the civil wars in Southern Rhodesia (Zimbabwe), Nigeria (the Biafran war) and Sri Lanka (between Tamils and Singhalese). Having only the power of truth, and otherwise being completely unarmed, pacifists are sometimes able to have dialogue directly with commanders of armed forces including terrorists. More often pacifists can do little during a hot war apart from rendering humanitarian assistance to its victims and encouraging governments in their peacemaking efforts towards ceasefires.

Such initiatives may involve the pacifist in compromise; but it is not for the sake of compromise that they are undertaken. The ultimate motivation remains intact – in Peter Jarman's words, 'to help create a society in which Hitlers and Stalins cannot assume power', or in those of George

Fox, to live 'in the virtue of that life and power that takes away the occasion of all wars'[17] and to witness to the possibility of human flourishing without recourse to violence or the threat of war. This is a hope to which the twentieth century, despite all its violence, has added a new degree of credibility. As we have seen, the United Nations, international institutions and conventions, international law, public awareness of the dangers created by the arms trade – these and other factors have been shown to have at least the potential to prevent or resolve conflicts without recourse to violence. The destructiveness of modern weapons is another possible reason (paradoxically) for believing major wars to be less likely: no responsible government would subject its citizens to the risk of decimation by massive retaliation. One analyst has recently expressed the hope that 'the worst of war is behind us' and that human kind 'will henceforth be able to conduct the affairs of the world in a way that allows war a diminishing part'.[18] Some would say even that economic globalization is potentially a positive factor, replacing the dangerously assertive policies of individual nations by the shared interests of multi-national companies and international agencies of economic development. Not that these new factors justify any easy optimism. The plague of second-hand weapons, particularly small arms, throughout the developing world has greatly exacerbated the suffering caused by local wars; the rise of dictatorships and the resurgence of xenophobic nationalism have caused the international community to mobilize massive armed forces and have largely neutralized the 'peace dividend' which seemed to be promised at the end of the Cold War; the continuing failure of the developed world to redress the scandalous imbalance of trade and wealth between north and south has left intact many of the long-term causes of war; and some would say (though there are good reasons for doubting it[19]) that the inevitable 'clash of civilizations', fuelled by increasingly fundamentalist religions and jealously-guarded cultures, will lead the world inexorably to the brink of major and possibly terminal war. Yet, on balance, the pacifist hope for a world without war and the pacifist witness to the possibilities of the non-violent resolution of conflict have if anything gained in credibility and in influence during the last half-century.

But for the Christian pacifist it is never merely a matter of assessing the grounds for hope and calculating the pragmatic advantages of non-violence over violence. Pacifists may still be in a minority among Christians; but their witness is a vital sign of human possibilities that God intends us to realize and of the radical imperative to work for peace, whatever the cost, which is laid upon us all. The analogy with monasticism is important in this context. Jesus' teaching on personal poverty and detachment from worldly possessions, combined with the call to self-sacrificial love inherent in the Christian faith, presents a radical and unambiguous challenge to every Christian. Yet the majority, in view of social and family responsibilities, the need to participate in the economic life of society, and a proper concern for the security and well-being of relatives and dependants, have felt bound to compromise with the way of the world and relegate Jesus' challenge to the level of a veto on extravagance or self-indulgence in their personal lifestyle and an incitement to charitable giving. Against this scenario of worldly compromise stands the historic witness of the monastic life, itself not without ambiguities and practical advantages (such as the assurance of care in old age), but with a clear renunciation (through the vow of poverty) of any personal striving for money, possessions and security. This witness represents a sign of at least the possibility of responding to Jesus' radical teaching, and has been shown again and again to liberate the individual for a life of worship and service which may approximate more nearly to that demanded by Christ than is normally possible for those who have not opted for this dedicated way of life. But it remains necessarily (not least because it normally demands celibacy) the way of a minority. It could never become a pattern for the whole church; yet without it a precious sign would be lost of the possibility of a whole-hearted response to Jesus' 'strenuous commands'[20] and of the serious hope of a kingdom on earth in which men and women may live in freedom from preoccupation with material possessions. Similarly the pacifist option, though it too has its own ambiguities and compromises, nevertheless holds before us all a clear sign of the possibility of a whole-hearted response to Jesus' teaching on non-retaliation and of a life in which love of one's neighbour is never negated by the deliberate use of violence. Even if it remains a minority response, without it the church could lose its vision of the human society which is intended by God and of which the achievements of pacifist action offer a precious foretaste.

For this, after all, was one of the most distinctive marks of Jesus' own teaching. Characteristically, he did not try to introduce an entirely new ethic. He did not make moral demands that had never been heard before. Rather, he drew attention again and again to actions of generosity and self-sacrificial service instinctively performed by (sometimes) the most unlikely people – a Samaritan, a spurned father, even an 'unjust judge' – and challenged his followers to do as much or even more as a sign of the potential which lies within the human spirit to respond to God's call and to live in a society – the kingdom – where such behaviour would be the norm. Similarly, the pacifist response to Jesus' call to non-violence is not an invitation to unnatural or super-human conduct, but evokes an instinctive human revulsion against the use of force, reminds us of the futility of the spiral of violence that is the curse of Cain, and stirs us to share the hope, in some ways more realistic today than ever before, of the coming of a kingdom in which war shall be no more.

In conclusion, we may return to the Bible for a more precise formulation of that hope.

Epilogue: The Message of the Apocalypse

In common usage the word 'apocalyptic' has acquired a negative and threatening connotation. We are alarmed by 'apocalyptic' forecasts of ecological disaster, we describe the horrors of a nuclear war as an 'apocalyptic scenario'. Certainly there are scenes and warnings in the biblical apocalypses, particularly that of St John, which are strong enough to make one's blood run cold and which justify the reputation of 'apocalyptic' for offering only a prospect of calamity. But these warnings were not written merely to dismay; however preoccupied they may seem to be with the reality of evil and the seriousness of the threats to humanity, they express also a deep conviction that there are grounds for encouragement, confidence and hope. This is particularly the case in Christian apocalyptic; but to appreciate this we need to understand the author's purpose and the idiom in which he wrote.

The 'Apocalypse' (or 'Revelation') of John', which stands at the end of the New Testament, is also described by the author as a 'prophecy' (1.3). This is a clue to its interpretation. Biblical scholars are accustomed to making a distinction between 'prophecy' and 'apocalyptic', – a modern term, derived from the Greek word meaning 'revelation'. By 'apocalyptic', they mean that class of writing which (though it was presaged in the great prophets) began in earnest with the Book of Daniel in the third century BCE and gave rise to a large number of Jewish books right up to the New Testament period. These look different from 'prophecy', in that their range is world-wide (not merely national, as in the prophets), their time-scale is one that leads up to the final culmination of history (not merely to the next historical crisis), their texture is composed of frequent allusions to the classical prophets and their theme is the revelation of the purposes which God has for the world, as imparted to one who has been vouchsafed privileged visions of 'what must be hereafter'.

It is clear that John's 'apocalypse' belongs in this category and has the same characteristics. Why then does he call it a 'prophecy', a genre from which modern scholars are so keen to distinguish it? The answer is, of course, that the distinction was unknown to him. However useful it may be to us – and there are certainly important differences between the two genres – we must not let it prevent us from seeing the similarities and indeed the essential continuity between them. Apocalyptic, certainly, has broadened the scope and sharpened the tension. It can accommodate a greater richness of imagery, symbolism and dramatic episode. But it uses many of the same resources as prophecy, and sets itself a similar task: to alert its readers to the wider significance of their contemporary history and to give such warnings or reassurances as are entailed by its understanding of current and future events. Prophecy, of course, always implies some claims to read off the future from the present. But this is not by any means its whole function. Old Testament scholars used to teach their pupils to think of the prophets, not as 'foretelling', but as 'forth-telling'. The great prophets of the Bible were not so much predicting what will happen as warning of the consequences of things going on as they are and urging their hearers to change their minds before it was too late. The apocalyptist may have enlarged the canvas and raised the stakes: it is now the future of the world, not just of the nation, which is in jeopardy. But, as we shall see, the object is still to influence people's conduct and thereby to avert catastrophe. What we call 'apocalyptic' still has all the moral weight and urgency of 'prophecy'.

It is this prophetic element of moral challenge which makes it impossible to read John's apocalypse as a kind of coded scenario of present or future history. The writer, certainly, claims to have been given privileged information on 'what must take place hereafter' (4.1). But this does not enable him to unroll the film of history forwards, as it were, and read off from it a series of particular events that must inevitably take place. His descriptions of the future are expressed in symbolic imagery, and have a vagueness and generality that would always make it difficult to know exactly whether and when they have been 'fulfilled'. This open-endedness of prediction (such that there is always doubt about what event the writer exactly meant) is again characteristic of Old Testament prophecy. To take a very familiar example: when Isaiah prophesied that 'a virgin shall conceive' (7.14), his original words meant no more than that a young woman would have a son – that is, there would be a particular birth – and that this would be a turning point in history. In the event, no 'birth' seems to have taken place which had such significance until Christians, seizing upon one possible meaning of a particular word ('young woman'/'virgin') saw the birth of Christ as the event in which the prophet's words seemed to have their fulfilment. The same was true even when a prophet appeared to fore-tell an event which actually came to pass in his own time. Later readers were unwilling to believe that this was all the prophecy 'meant': prophecies continued to be meditated on as meaningful indications of the tendencies of history and as warnings or reassurances for the faithful. St John's 'prophecy', therefore, was not to be expected to be definitively fulfilled in the events of his own or even some future period of history. It was deliberately expressed in a form that would be seen to be a recognizable portrayal of contemporary historical events but would also have a generality that would allow other events and other periods to be equally a 'fulfilment' of it. Above all, it shared with the classical prophets the same moral urgency. If you believe, as some Christians claim to do, that the book can be decoded in such a way that it will reveal the outlines of future history and tell us exactly what is destined to happen, then only one response is possible: make sure you are one of those who will be 'saved' from the predicted catastrophes and conduct your personal life accordingly. But John's apocalypse, like true prophecy, demands a more serious response than this. Certainly it is predictive: this is the kind of thing that, in present circumstances, is bound to happen. But how fatal its consequences will be for humanity, and whether it will lead to still further destruction, is the responsibility of human beings. The ultimate denouement is *not* certain: it depends on our response to the prophecy.

Let us spend a moment considering the circumstances in which John wrote. He tells us that he was 'on the island called Patmos because I had preached God's word and borne my testimony to Jesus' (1.9), which is usually taken to mean that he was there in exile or captivity. The monastery which today marks the traditional site of his sojourn provides a likely setting. From Patmos, St John could look over the sea to the coastline of Asia Minor. Within a radius of a hundred miles on the mainland there were seven cities, each of which had a small Christian congregation. The Christian movement was as yet on a minute scale compared with the overwhelming cultural and political influence wielded by imperial Rome. Yet a part of John's revelation was to see this incipient movement as nevertheless the crucial factor in the historical development of the entire Mediterranean world (the only 'world' he knew). The witness, the suffering and the commitment to peace and brotherly love of the first few generations of Christians seemed to him to be the tiny fulcrum on which the destiny of all was poised. We may call it (for its time at least) a grandiose claim. Yet it has never been proved false; and (as we have seen) it still has plausibility and power.

John describes himself as one who shares with those whom he addresses 'the tribulation and the kingdom and the endurance in Jesus' (1.9). His choice of words is significant. Today, when we are confronted by a threatening turn of events, we call it a 'crisis'. The implication is that, if it is properly 'managed', it will pass, and things will return to normal. But this is not how the first generations of Christians viewed the trials and the tribulations to which they were subjected. They never imagined that these were 'crises' that might have been avoided or that would blow over in due course. On the contrary, 'tribulation' was a necessary aspect of life seen from the Christian perspective. God does not intend us to have an easy time. Conditions will always be such that we shall have to pay a heavy price for our convictions and our faith in terms of vigilance, constancy and personal sacrifice. The gift that is fundamental to all our Christian existence (and which John takes for granted in his readers as in himself) is. 'endurance'. Only this makes it realistic to think that we shall ever have experience of 'the kingdom' – the state of affairs in which love and persuasion prevail over force, and in which that peace is established which is not as the world gives and which, as we have seen, is the fruit of costly and sustained endeavour. St John, confronted by the sufferings of his fellow-Christians and alerted to the signs of those endemic tendencies in human society that break out in aggression, destruction and oppression, lays down the presuppositions of any creatively

Christian response, namely acceptance of tribulation, with all the Christian resources of endurance, in view of the possibility of a totally different state of affairs: the state of genuine God-given peace – the kingdom.

Of the many images that John uses to describe the recurrent catastrophes of history, the Four Horsemen of chapter 6 have passed most easily into the currency of our language and our imagination. Like all his images, they resist precise identification. The first two – one with a bow and the crown of victory, the other with a great sword – are conventionally interpreted as war and civil strife; the remaining two are less ambiguous: famine and death. Between them, they are capable of representing all the consequences of the endlessly indulged human propensity to the use of force, violence and warfare. No particular sequence of events will ever precisely 'fulfil' this prophecy: it stands as an imaginative tableau representing all such conflicts. These are the forces which (against all reason) are recurrently unleashed to settle human disputes. Yet there is also a restraint. 'But do not damage the olive and the vine' (6.6). A basic instinct for survival endures even through the most savage conflicts. The slow-growing vines and olives were to be spared from the ravages of war. The restraint was not absolute: every olive tree within miles had been razed by the Romans in their siege of Jerusalem not many years before John can be presumed to have been writing. But as a general description of warfare the restriction rings true. A scorched earth strategy is seldom justified; victors as well as victims require the resources of the earth. Even in the field of nuclear weaponry there is a perceived value in being (were it possible) 'ecologically clean'.

This, then, is the character of John's dramatic images: they are sharp enough to arouse alarm and stir the imagination, but they have also the ambivalence and generality that allows them to stand for each successive horror that passing

generations inflict on one another. Of course one may detect
the influence of particular events on the mind of the writer.
When he writes

> What looked like a great mountain flaming with fire was
> hurled into the sea; a third of the sea was turned to blood,
> a third of the living creatures in it died, and a third of
> the ships on it were destroyed (8.8–9)

he may well have been moved by reports of the eruption of
Vesuvius which engulfed Pompeii in 79 CE. Again, when he
described the release of 'the four angels who are bound at
the great river Euphrates', and observed that

> the power of the horses lay in their mouths and in their
> tails; for their tails had heads like serpents, and with them
> they inflicted injuries (9.19)

there can be little doubt that he had in mind the dreaded
Parthian cavalry, which were famous for their tactic of
shooting their arrows at the enemy when galloping away
from him. Indeed this illustration is of more than passing
significance. The Parthians themselves had become a symbol
of the ever-present barbarian threat to Graeco-Roman civilization. Successive Roman generals had attempted to con-
quer them and failed. Their armies were known to be poised
at the eastern-most frontier of the Roman empire, the Euphrates. The threat of a savage invasion from that quarter
inspired a general anxiety that belied the alleged security of
the *pax Romana*. There was even a superstitious fear abroad
that Nero (whose disappearance had been mysterious) might
turn out to be in hiding, preparing to reconquer his empire
at the head of the Parthian armies. We can see here precisely
that process of depersonalization which is one of the most
dangerous features of long-range and highly-destructive

missiles today: the enemy, being distant and unknown, is described in impersonal, almost symbolic terms, and comes to present a threat against which any form of pre-emptive attack or retaliation seems justified. Out of this particular instance St John has made another symbol of enduring application.

John's apoclypse is a series of seven-fold visions, each adding something to the last, but each self-contained in itself. It is clear that we must not read them as a temporal progression of calamities, as if these things were to take place one after the other. So great are the casualties from the first two that there would not be enough human beings left to sustain the sequences that follow! Each vision is more like a re-play of a previous one, a fresh imagining of the horrors in store for civilized human beings; and already at the end of the second the writer is eager to offer us his disturbing conclusion from his reading of human history:

> The rest of mankind, who survived these plagues, still did not renounce the gods their hands had made, or cease their worship of demons and of idols . . . nor did they repent of their murders, their sorcery, their fornication, or their robberies (9.20–21).

John had already witnessed or heard reports of war, violence, corruption and oppression that gave him ample material for his visions of the future; but he had also observed – and this is the moral thrust of his whole project – that the suffering and destruction caused by each act of aggression, domination or rebellion was never enough to deter human kind from entering the deadly cycle of violence all over again. The First World War was fought with such reckless and apparently uncontrollable expenditure of human life and suffering that many believed that modern war had become too terrible ever to be waged again. The author of Revelation knew better. Even then, human beings had not 'repented of the works of their hands' and were soon ready to go to war once more. The same is true today. Nuclear war has become too horrible to contemplate. But none of us can afford to assume that we will 'repent of the works of our hands'. John's reading of history remains as valid for our time as for his.

What then is our hope? Let us read on a few chapters. The visions continue with renewed ferocity. Various beasts are allowed to exercise their ruthless dominion over the earth – they may stand for Roman emperors, but again the symbolism is open-ended: their relevance is not exhausted by any particular embodiment. By now the death-toll of plagues, battles, famines, earthquakes and persecutions has reached devastating proportions; if we were to take the descriptions literally we would have to say that civilization was at an end, the environment damaged beyond repair, and all sources of hope extinguished. But then we read:

> Then I saw an angel flying in midheaven with an eternal gospel to proclaim to those on earth ... 'Fear God and pay him homage, for the hour of his judgment has come! Worship him ...' This calls for the endurance of God's people, all those who keep his commands and remain loyal to Jesus (14.6–7, 12).

The words to dwell on are 'an eternal gospel'. We have felt already the moral thrust of John's reading of history: the consequences of their own follies, however calamitous, will not persuade human kind to change course, renounce war and pursue justice. But into this bleak situation God has introduced a further factor: the gospel is *eternal*, the chance is *always* there, it is *never* too late to turn back and forsake our evil ways and begin to 'fear God and give him glory' – which is John's shorthand for a life (of a society as well as of individuals) which is lived in conformity with God's directives and which begins to reveal, not the catastrophic scale of human pretensions, but the splendour and beauty of the Creator as displayed in the free response of his creatures to the intimations of his loving and peaceful purposes. We often say, 'it would mean a change of heart', meaning, 'it is impossible'. The eternal gospel is the promise that a change of heart is possible, is indeed already a reality in the lives of those who have responded to the astonishing revelation that God's nature is to be known, not through a conquering Messiah, but through 'a Lamb with the marks of sacrifice on him' (5.6). This, and this only, is the ground of our hope; it is a 'call for the endurance of the saints'. Nothing can, or could, ever happen to make this 'gospel', this promise, invalid.

John's reading of history, then, was utterly realistic. He had no illusions about human nature; the *pax Romana* under which he lived revealed itself as a precarious security founded on deception, acquisitiveness and idolatry; and he saw no reason to think that humanity, unaided, would ever establish a better world order. Self-destruction seemed the ineluctable consequence of recurrent patterns of human self-aggrandisement. He appears to have been quite unimpressed by the standards of administration and justice set up in the Roman provinces or by the apparent security obtained by Roman military superiority; none of these can he have thought sufficient to divert the inevitable consequences of excessive affluence and power. We can imagine that he would have been equally sceptical of the power of a nuclear threat to deter the outbreak of hostilities today. Yet along with this realism went an unassailable confidence. God had revealed an alternative way and, in Christ, had given men and women the resources to follow it. This was not a 'way out', an invitation to withdraw from the scene of conflict and maintain a kind of spiritual isolation from its effects.

On the contrary, it was 'a call to endurance', a summons to continue to proclaim an eternal gospel, to witness to the ever-present possibility of a change of heart by living *as if* it was already coming to pass. The tribulation that Christians must endure was no accident; it was not an unfortunate period of reverses that might soon pass. It was the necessary condition of their commitment to a better state of affairs, it was the price they must always be ready to pay for their vision, their confidence that, one day, there will be 'peace'.

But where does John ever speak about peace? Is his book not taken up with descriptions of the terrible alternative to peace? It is true that he never once uses the word. But his final vision is of Jerusalem (whose name meant 'city of peace'), re-established by God in circumstances symbolic of peace – its gates shall never be shut by day (21.25). In that city – which has come down out of heaven from God (21.2, 19), and so is not a human creation, its peace is not 'as the world gives' – the conditions of life are such that the Greek word for 'peace' would be inadequate; only the Hebrew *shalom* would do them justice. It is a city in which the dream of both Jewish and Christian faith is realized: 'Now God has his dwelling with mankind!' (21.3). Religion is no longer a matter of temple or church, but a spontaneous recognition of the constant presence of God, conformity to his will and celebration of his glory (21.22–23); and all this is no preserve of any sect or religion, but is in the service of the whole of humanity: 'by its light shall the nations walk . . . the leaves of the trees (of life) are for the healing of the nations' (21.24; 22.2). The *shalom* of the new Jerusalem is the hope of the whole world. And yet it remains true that *there is no peace for the wicked*: 'nothing unclean shall enter, nor anyone whose ways are foul or false' (21.27). The vision is no sentimental scenario of a *deus ex machina* somehow making everything perfect for everyone. The City of Peace is only for the worshippers of the true God. But its regime now extends to 'the nations'; the forces of love and persuasion are now in the ascendant. And for those who persist in their old ways there is still 'the eternal gospel'. The chance of repentance is always there, which is the passport for admission through the ever-open gates of the holy city.

We are led, by this route, to a mystery. Before it, we stand humbled and amazed. The peace of God 'passes all understanding' – necessarily, since its social expression is beyond the scope of any human institution and the intensity of worshipful interdependence it presupposes has rarely been experienced on this earth. Yet it is no distant ideal or utopia. It is something we must promote by our faithfulness and for which we are called to endure. Peacemaking is costly. It is a commitment we can and must assume as part of our Christian discipleship. Even the world's peace can be had only at a price, a price Christians, if anyone, should be ready to pay. But the peace of God – peace 'not as the world gives' – is nothing less than the perfect expression of our faith in a social mode, the establishment of the new Jerusalem on earth. Such a peace is not just a high priority. It is the vision which gives meaning to our lives, power to our prayers, hope and endurance in the midst of our history. It is the sum of all we believe, all we strive for, all we pray for as we seek to respond to the promise of God's kingdom on earth.

Appendix

Nuclear Pacifism in the Post-Cold War World

Brian Wicker

Introduction

'Would you press the button you know is going to annihilate millions of people?'

'If the circumstances demanded it, I would.'

This reply, given under oath by Air Commodore Magill to Pat Pottle at the British Official Secrets Trial of February 1962, distilled the essence of Cold War nuclear deterrence (as Walter Stein pointed out at the time).[1] The Air Commodore was merely confirming what the nuclear deterrers of the 1960s had always claimed: namely that nuclear forces 'present to any attacker the prospect of virtual annihilation of his country'.[2] Of course, because of the outrageousness and even incredibility of such threats, nuclear strategy was later modified, notably during Robert McNamara's tenure as Secretary of Defense, by introducing graduated threats short of outright annihilation, to meet lesser contingencies. It was claimed this was done by targeting 'the enemy's military forces, not his civilian population' in order to give 'a possible opponent the strongest possible incentive to refrain from attacking our own cities'.[3] Yet, despite the apparent moral advance represented by these moves, it was always insisted that the power to destroy the enemy's cities, and if necessary to annihilate his whole society, remained and had to remain as the ultimate sanction. 'We must assure that the missile force is completely reliable and can be depended upon to destroy absolutely the Soviet Union even after we absorb a surprise attack.'[4]

Whatever we may think of the wisdom of such a strategy, the wickedness of what it consents to cannot be denied. It envisages committing exactly the 'crime against God and Man' which the Second Vatican Council, with nuclear deterrence very much in mind, had condemned unequivocally and without hesitation in 1965.[5] Yet even today, with the Cold War over and in a quite new set of global circumstances, some people in a few countries still hanker after nuclear weapons for purposes of national security. So the question is: can a nuclear deterrence plan be formulated for post-Cold War circumstances, which decisively, unambiguously and unhesitatingly repudiates all thought of such crimes? And even if such a plan could be reliably formulated in theory, could it be adopted in practice? And even if it could, has it actually been adopted by any nuclear weapons state? And even if such a state did so adopt it, could we rely on its being adhered to, come hell or high water, in the midst of mounting anger and panic during a crisis? In short, given that the commission of 'city-bashing' crimes became routine in the Second World War, can we be certain that political and military leaders in the future would abjure the temptation to commit them once again? Have we been given sufficient assurances by governments that such crimes could and would never again be contemplated, however great the temptation?

Nuclear pacifists have long said no to every one of these questions.[6] On the other hand, 'principled possessionists'[7] today insist on saying yes to some if not all of them. Which of the two is right?

This question is of crucial importance in Britain today because, in addition to committing itself in its election manifesto to the elimination of nuclear weapons, the Blair government has also committed itself to the retention of British nuclear weapons for the next thirty years. Whether this twin-track policy makes consistent sense can only be adequately discussed by a close examination of the case presented. Meanwhile, the policy persists against the background of two contrasting facts. The first is that many of those who have been involved in the development of nuclear weapons recognize that there is now, for a limited time, the opportunity to get rid of them. Expert international groups are pressing this case ever more strongly.[8] What is more, they recognize the dangers of not doing so. First of all, as long as nuclear weapons remain in existence the possibility of their being used in anger or by mischance also exists; a possibility perhaps almost amounting in the end to certainty.[9] Secondly, classical nuclear deterrence (if there can be such a thing)[10] is breaking down in a world which is no longer dominated by bi-polar mutual hostility. Hence the probability that nuclear weapons will spread to new areas of the world, especially among states which feel insecure. Thirdly, the danger of acquisition and use by the disaffected or fanatical, whether 'rogue' states or non-state groups, is increasing. Furthermore it is hard to see how nuclear weapons held by the declared nuclear states can act as effective deterrents against them.[11] Fourthly, in the light of these considerations, negotiations for a global treaty to ban nuclear weapons, with an effective monitoring and verification regime, are becoming acceptable to many states.[12] Meanwhile nuclear weapons become less prominent in the policies of those states which have long possessed them. In short, there is today a window of opportunity to rid the world of a 'scourge'[13] which, if not eliminated, may well destroy us all.

Yet, ironically, at just this moment, public awareness of and interest in these dangers is at an all-time low. The mass public campaigns of the early 1980s have disappeared. The end of the Cold War has caused public opinion to take up new challenges instead: anti-personnel landmines, small and light weapons, ecological problems. The result is that just at the moment when there is a chance of serious nuclear disarmament leading to complete elimination, governments, especially in the developed world, even when officially committed to the goal of abolition, have little incentive to do anything serious about it. Furthermore, the Comprehensive Test Ban Treaty has had the unfortunate effect of calming public fears and apprehensions, and thus of contributing to an apathy which disguises the dangers of doing nothing. Hence the importance of opinion-forming bodies, such as the churches, keeping up their pressure for action while the opportunity to avoid catastrophe still exists.

Nuclear Pacifism

The term 'nuclear pacifism' describes an absolute and unconditional rejection of nuclear weapons and nuclear policy, while not necessarily rejecting the possibility that some other forms of armed conflict might remain just. It is ultimately based on two fundamental principles, one ethical and the other legal. The ethical principle is that it is never licit intentionally to kill innocent human beings in order to gain some end, however good. Nuclear pacifists are convinced that the policy of deterrence necessarily includes, as a last resort if not before, a willingness, or conditional intention, to commit such an act; or at the very least entails consent to its being committed. They believe, for reasons already sketched briefly above, that the nuclear powers have always of necessity been committed to the possibility, however remote, of having to undertake acts of war aimed indiscriminately at the destruction of entire cities or extensive areas along with their population.[14]

The legal principle is that not every form of armed defence is allowed by international law. Various conventions, subsumed under the general title of 'the humanitarian laws of war', already outlaw certain kinds of behaviour.[15] Nuclear pacifists believe that the policy of nuclear deterrence, with its unavoidable commitment, at some stage of escalation, to breach of these laws, is *ipso facto* illegal; and that the conditional intentions involved in deterrence are therefore intentions to commit illegal acts. The fact that NATO exists partly to defend the principle of the rule of law[16] makes the illegality of the accompanying deterrent intentions on the part of the NATO states particularly egregious.

Principled Possessionism

The first thing to say about 'principled possessionism' is that preventing war and the horrors and crimes associated with it are the principled possessionist's overriding ambition.[17] Furthermore, the principled possessionist may well feel more confident that his aim can be achieved by retaining nuclear weapons (in the hands of only a few 'reliable' states) than the principled nuclear disarmer is of his attaining the same end by the nuclear disarmament route. But what is over-riding for the nuclear disarmer is the need to expunge from the international mind all thought of mass-murderousness as a means of preventing war, while avoiding nuclear disaster in the longer term.

The key thesis of 'principled possessionists' is simple: nuclear deterrence is still the best available means for preventing war between major states. This is because nuclear weapons have ushered in a 'Copernican revolution' in international affairs, by which the very idea of a nuclear weapons state going to war to gain a political objective against another nuclear weapons state has become utterly irrational. Indeed nuclear deterrence is the *reductio ad absurdum* of war itself. This 'Copernican revolution' in human affairs is irreversible because the know-how to build a nuclear deterrent can never be erased. Humanity has henceforth to live not only with the nuclear secret, but with its political and military consequences. It follows that from now on, in conflicts between nuclear weapon states, there can be no such thing as a military victory in the classical sense: that is, a feat of arms in which the adversary's capacity to inflict further harm on us is destroyed. All a state can hope for in the nuclear era is to mount a threat which will force an attacker to back off before it is too late; i.e. to persuade him to deal with mutual differences in some non-military way. (Deterrence is simply an irresistibly coercive means of 'dissuasion', as the French are always at pains to point out.)

The Copernican Revolution Examined

Unfortunately, human beings have not yet succeeded in matching the Copernican revolution in military technology with an equivalent revolution in moral or political understanding. The debate about nuclear weapons, both for and against, is still mostly conducted by means of old thinking. Ethical criteria drawn from the 'Ptolemaic' era of warfare are commonly deployed as if they still made sense in the post-Copernican age. Whether they believe it to be morally outrageous or morally legitimate many people continue to talk as if nuclear war were still a serious last resort option. This is not surprising. For the old notions about war, and how it can be won, are still enormously attractive, and very profoundly ingrained.[18] Consider how satisfying to many in the liberal democracies is the claim that the West 'won' the Cold War – and how deeply-felt in Russia is the sense of having 'lost' it! As long as states are in conflict with one another, they will surely continue, even in the nuclear era, to imagine that if only they had the will and the means, they could achieve victory over their adversaries. The United Nations Charter itself is built on this assumption, in its legitimation of the rights of nations to go to war in self-defence.[19] This is why the Nuclear Non-Proliferation Treaty was a rewriting of the UN Charter for the nuclear age, because in Article VI it de-legitimized the nuclear arms race which the old thinking by major states necessarily embodied (see below). [20]

More important still, the dozens of major wars that have taken place during the nuclear era itself are compelling evidence of the persistence of old thinking in the new age – and surely with good reason. For the Copernican revolution has only touched the major states, especially the nuclear states and their allies.[21] In short, nuclear deterrence hardly affects the many real wars that have happened in the nuclear age. To the average participant in such wars, wielding his Kalashnikov or his AK47, nuclear deterrence exists only among far-away countries of which he knows nothing. For his leaders, nuclear deterrence has not reduced war to absurdity at all.

But there is a more profound problem even than this. It was succinctly put by Pope Paul VI speaking to the United Nations in 1978 during the bi-polar Cold War era: 'The logic underlying the request for the balance of power impels each of the adversaries to seek to ensure a certain margin of superiority, for fear of being left at a disadvantage.'[22] In other words, even in a condition of 'balanced' deterrence, or 'mutually assured destruction', a nuclear arms race is unavoidable, because of the felt political and psychological need to be in a position to win, or at least not to lose, the contest. This point is made even more forcibly by General Lee Butler, who was responsible for many years during the Cold War for turning nuclear strategy into workable military plans:

Deterrence, when raised to its highest level, requires that you make yourself effectively invulnerable to an enemy's attack. In the nuclear age, the requirements are especially high, because the consequences of even one nuclear weapon slipping through your defences are going to be catastrophic. Yet your perfect invulnerability would spell perfect vulnerability for your opponent, which of course he cannot accept. Consequently, any balance struck is extremely unstable, and each side is led to build larger and larger arsenals, to discover more and more elegant technologies. Yet these never strike the desired balance either.[23]

In other words, deterrence is never stable, even though it may be 'robust'.[24] In short, the Cold War competition to acquire excessive numbers of nuclear warheads was no aberration; it was simply a corollary of mutual deterrence itself.

The Reductio ad Absurdum *of Nuclear Possession*

Yet principled possessionists continue to pin their hopes on deterrence, perhaps indefinitely, but at a lower level of salience than it acquired during the Cold War.[25] At the same time all thought of 'city bashing' and the obliteration of combatant/non-combatant distinctions, that predecessors in the tradition thought so necessary for its effectivenness, have to be expunged.[26] But even if this could be done without fatally damaging the whole idea of effective deterrence, it is anyhow far from clear that the project of a stable state of deterrence between nuclear powers at a steady, low level of salience is practically sustainable in the long-term.[27] For it presupposes that the states concerned have already made the 'Copernican' leap to a new way of thinking in which trying for old style 'victory' by superiority of nuclear power has already been abandoned. But if such a state of tacit co-operation in thinking by opposing states has already been achieved, why is deterrence and its threat of ultimate sanction needed to insure against its failure? The scenario seems to be self-contradictory. It postulates a contest (between, say, a re-militarized Russia and the West) in which both players have already agreed in advance not to try to win, but rather to back off at a certain point short of winning. For if they have not in advance agreed to do this, then the weaker will surely find itself constrained in the early stages of the crisis to return to the unavoidable nuclear arms racing that Paul VI and General Butler have drawn attention to, because the backing off will only come, *ex hypothesi*, through coercion by means of superior nuclear threats. How is the weaker adversary to recognize that he must back off unless and until he has tried (and failed) to win the contest by mounting a superior coercive threat?

Beyond this, however, lies a yet more profound conundrum. Since the end of the Cold War America has emerged as the sole superpower. It is using the post-Cold War period, before the emergence of any potential rivals, to achieve 'full spectrum dominance' by the use of its superiority in military technology for all conceivable scenarios. This form of dominance aims to make the United States invulnerable to defeat in war in any part of the world, on land, sea and air (and in outer space) by any possible adversary. Part of this programme for military dominance in defence of US national interests involves the institutionalization of nuclear deterrence – apparently without any regard for the legality or otherwise of nuclear threats and use – by means of 'modernized' nuclear warheads. These are being developed and tested in American nuclear weapons laboratories, circumventing any limitations laid down by the Comprehensive Test Ban Treaty, in order to make nuclear deterrence, and even nuclear war-fighting, a practical possibility, not merely against nuclear-armed opponents but against Third World possessors of chemical and biological weapons. The 'Copernican revolution' in thinking about war does not seem to have penetrated the most advanced centres of weapons development in the most advanced country of the world.[28]

Principled Possessionism Examined

We have no experience of war conducted between nuclear-armed adversaries. So we do not know for certain what it would be like. This means that arguments about its likely implications have to take the form of rational estimates of probabilities. These have to be based on experience of older forms of conflict; on theoretical and scientific models of nuclear war (including computer simulations, war-games etc.); on the destructive potentialities of the weapons involved; on the known or assumed intentions and mind-sets of those taking the crucial decisions; etc. In other words, nuclear deterrence is a form of insurance policy, or calculated gamble. But we cannot be certain that this gamble will succeed – or that it will fail.

Deterrence cannot be mere bluff: it must include a certain willingness to regard the use of nuclear weapons in anger as a genuine option. But principled possessionism goes further by insisting that such use must conform to two principles: (a) the harm done in the non-military sphere must not be disproportionate to the legitimate military objective; (b) the war must not be waged through attack on the innocent. The question then arises, how to square these key principles with the fact that nuclear deterrence has to include the final sanction of an ultimate strategic strike. For without this the whole deterrence structure unravels.[29] Part of the answer given to this conundrum is that while there is always a theoretical possibility, in nuclear-age conflict, of escalation until the 'final sanction' is reached, such escalation is not automatic. On the contrary, the very first use of a nuclear weapon may well convince the adversaries that they share a common interest in solving their conflict in a non-military way.[30] Thus reassured, during the Cold War principled possessionism could continue to hold that the risk of catastrophic escalation was worth taking because of the gravity of the issues involved and the immensity of the gains that may be had from the successful maintenance of deterrence. But not every commentator agreed with this assessment.[31]

The rights or wrongs of this disagreement may in the end be objectively undecidable. But in any case, the nub of the argument today is not about risk-assessment: it is about the *absolute* illicitness of *ever* directly or intentionally killing the innocent, whether in war or in any other context.[32] One way out of this difficulty would be to show that final-sanction nuclear-strike plans could be worked out which would remain within the spirit of the Just War tradition. In other words, deterrence can be retained without the commitment to 'city-bashing', let alone total annihilation of the enemy society, which used to be regarded as essential to the 'final sanction'.

Unfortunately this answer is far from adequate. For it is necessary to keep to the letter as well as the spirit of the Just War tradition, especially the 'letter' of the apodictic prohibition on intentionally, or consentingly, killing the innocent. Not only must we in no circumstances intend, however conditionally, to kill innocent non-combatants; we have no right voluntarily to consent to their being killed in order to achieve our end.[33] Keeping casualties among innocent citizens as low as possible is an admirable goal, but it is not enough. The principled deterrer has to ensure that these unavoidable deaths do not enter into his calculus of what he intends the adversary to fear.[34] That is to say innocent casualties have to be genuinely 'side effects', wholly unintended and accidental to our purpose. But there are good arguments to show that this is impossible; that is, there can be no 'final sanction' scenario which does not involve consent to the *intentional* killing of innocent non-combatants.

These arguments are presented in great detail by Finnis, Boyle and Grisez, and for an adequate appreciation of them the reader must turn to their book.[35] The principled deterrer's claim essentially is that it would be possible to deny an aggressor victory by using only 'pure counterforce' methods at the stage of the 'final sanction'. Finnis, Boyle and Grisez, however, mount a very powerful case for saying that a deterrent designed to deny the aggressor victory by using only 'pure counterforce' is impossible.[36]

Nevertheless theirs is only an argument drawn, by allegedly inexorable logic, from allegedly indisputable premisses. While it has great force for this reason, it is still an argument in the abstract, purporting to establish what *must* happen in the absence of actual experience. The principled possessionist would doubtless reply that this is just its weakness; we can never be quite as certain of how things will turn out as such an argument suggests. History is not logic. Things happen which sometimes subvert such rational clarities. So the argument is ultimately just another risk-assessment. What are the chances that things will go as the logic seems to dictate? Can we be so certain that the decision-makers on both sides would feel constrained in quite the way the argument suggests?

This point, however, is no refutation of the argument. For in the absence of proof in experience, principled possessionism has to show that the argument itself is invalid: but to my knowledge this has never been done. The possibility of avoiding the intentional killing of the innocent, e.g. by repudiating 'city-bashing' (but not of course the unavoidable lethal irradiation of the target area which will also cause innocent deaths) is commonly asserted;[37] but proof, in the shape of detailed plans for *making sure* that such destruction would be avoided in a crisis, is not available for inspection. Nor can it be; for revealing such plans would be fatal to the secrecy on which the whole deterrence-strategy depends. Anyhow we cannot be sure of what would happen in the future, and the history of the twentieth century gives us every reason to believe that, in the event, the moral barriers existing in military heads would be breached in the event of war. True, we are told, despite the actual history of nuclear strategy, that 'effective deterrence does not inescapably imply pure counter-population targeting'.[38] But we are in the dark about whether or how far such effective deterrence is even planned, let alone how it can be relied upon in the heat of violent conflict. Published work on the subject tends to avoid the key problem, putting enormous store by the hope that the adversaries would back off long before things got to the pass that the argument suggests. It also tends to claim that the remaining difficulties can be met by use of 'double effect', 'lesser of two evils' or similar reasonings.[39] But if principled possessionism is right, the application of such reasonings in the context of warfare has always rested on the prior abjuration of any consent or intention, however conditional, to kill the innocent in any circumstances. The main point of 'double effect' reasoning here is to permit the deaths of innocents as 'side-effects' while abjuring all intention to kill the innocent. Hence principled possessionism has to go on to claim that a plan which would be enough to deter could be devised without having in mind the option of massive attack on cities. But still this is not enough; we need to know that such a deterrence policy *has been put into effect and that it will work*. Has it? We have never been told.[40] Nor can we: for keeping the secret from the adversary entails keeping it from us, who are entitled to know. Anyhow, even if such a plan already exists, why should we feel any more confident that those responsible for carrying it out will hold to their moral scruples in a time of great future crisis than they did in World War Two, or in Vietnam? What assurance can we have that they can be trusted not to buckle under the almost intolerable pressure of future murderous temptations, when they have already buckled under them so often in this century?[41]

Of course even if the attacks were not consciously directed at the non-combatant population they would certainly kill a lot of non-combatants; and even if it were true that such non-combatant deaths could be 'proportionate' given the enormity of the inevitable alternative, e.g. Nazi or Stalinist world-conquest,[42] this would not dispose of the argument that they were still being used *as means to the end* of deterrence, namely the prevention of aggression. Some people might think them proportionate, given the alternative; but this does not dispose of the claim that they would nevertheless constitute intentional killings, that is murders.

Some commentators have tried to get round this difficulty by suggesting that the non-combatants in question are not really 'innocents'.[43] Others, having conceded that this escape-route is not open, claim that some level of intentional killing of the innocent is licit if the ultimate objective is sufficiently important.[44] But the principled possessionist cannot take either of these escape routes. The result is a temptation to build some kind of escape-hatch into the wording of the argument itself: nuclear deterrence does not entail attacking population *as such* or *per se*. But this kind of language does not disguise the fact that, while it helps to make deterrence seem more humanly acceptable, by disavowing targeting civilians 'as such', it retains the threat to civilians all the same.[45] As far as I know, there is no evidence available in the public realm that the mass-murderous deterrence strategy we knew in the early 1960s, together with all the weapons that made it possible, has been permanently abjured. If I am wrong, let us have the evidence. Who has said so? Where? And in what terms? There is certainly nothing about it in the 1998 Strategic Defence Review.

Ethics and International Law

A further consideration has to do with the observance of law. It is always a sigificant decision to disobey the law in a society in which the rule of law is a key value, both in theory and in practice.[46] Now in international law, nuclear deterrence is at best only doubtfully legal. The 8 July 1996 Advisory Opinion of the International Court of Justice, than which there is no higher source of international legal opinion, states quite clearly that 'the threat of or use of nuclear weapons would generally be contrary to the rules of international law applicable in armed conflict, and in particular the principles and rules of humanitarian law'. The only exception the Court considers is when there is a threat to the very survival of the state which is proposing to use, or is threatening to use, nuclear weapons. The ICJ was unable to conclude definitively whether in such cases the use of nuclear weapons would be lawful, or indeed whether the threat of their use as a deterrent would be lawful.[47]

How does the British Trident system fare under these constraints?

The ICJ points out in §78 of its Advisory Opinion that international humanitarian law forbids the use of any weapon which is incapable of distinguishing between civilian and military targets. A difficulty arises in the case of nuclear weapons because of their explosive yields and radiation effects. Since a nuclear weapon spreads radiation effects over a wide area, and because this radiation effect is part and parcel of any detonation of the bomb, it is arguable in law that the whole circle of territory affected by radiation must be recognized as constituting the area under attack. Furthermore, this radiation endures for a long time, thus preventing future uses of the land by civilians who may have had no part whatever in the original conflict. Hence (it is argued) any use of the bomb is unavoidably indiscriminate between military and civilian objects of attack both in space and in time.

If this argument holds then any use of the nuclear bomb is *ipso facto* illegal under humanitarian law. But may humanitarian law be legally trumped by considerations of military necessity in the case of the very survival of the state which uses the weapon? This is what *seems* to be at issue in the ICJ's one exception to its rule that all nuclear use or threat of use is generally illegal. But it is also clear that humanitarian law may *not* be trumped in this way. 'States must *never* make civilians the object of attack and must consequently *never* use weapons that are incapable of distinguishing between civilian and military targets.'[48] According to John Burroughs, an international lawyer closely involved in the process leading up to the publication of the Advisory Opinion, 'the severely restricted consequences of this fundamental constraint for the threat or use of nuclear weapons imply that even when the survival of a state acting in self-defence is at stake, uncertainty would arise with respect only to limited threats or uses like the postulated "clean" use of "low yield" nuclear weapons which the Court found the nuclear weapon states had not demonstrated to be legal but also did not expressly find to be illegal'.[49] It is true that the British government maintains a degree of flexibility in the choice of yield of its Trident warheads in order to allow for 'limited use'. This is part of what it means by a sub-strategic capability[50] designed to ensure 'that no nuclear armed aggressor could gamble on us being self-deterred from crossing the nuclear threshold in extreme circumstances of self-defence by fear of an inevitable strategic exchange'.[51] But of course, this does not remove the need to deploy much higher-yield weapons as well. This is because of the need to make execution of the 'final sanction' of a strategic nuclear exchange possible if this sub-strategic use does not after all deter the aggressor.

A further legal problem underlying the 'state's survival' exception to the general illegality of nuclear weapons is that the NATO nuclear states all propose to use their weapons in defence of their allies, as well as of themselves.[52] Is this legal under the ICJ Opinion? In §97 it is clearly stated that what is at issue here is 'the use of a nuclear weapon by a state in an extreme circumstance of self-defence, in which *its* very survival would be at stake'. This clearly limits the legal use of the weapon to the survival of the state using it, not to that of any other state, such as a NATO ally. However if, as might be argued, this wording is an unintentional slip, given that the *dispositif* of the Opinion does not quite commit itself to so narrow a circumscription,[53] the result would be the creation of two levels of self-defence for which different rules applied – something not allowed for under the UN Charter Article 51.[54]

Finally, the decision to keep nuclear weapons, and in particular the Trident system, for up to thirty years[55] would seem to be illegal in view of the ICJ's clear stipulation that 'there exists an obligation to pursue in good faith and bring to a conclusion negotiations leading to nuclear disarmament in all its aspects under strict and effective international control'.[56] While the Court does not demand a timetable for these negotiations, the failure of the UK even to hint at a target date for negotiations to begin, together with its repeated votes against UN resolutions which stipulate an early start,[57] suggests at the very least that the UK is deliberately ignoring, if not actually breaking, international law at this point.

The above discussion of the legal problem of Britain's nuclear deterrent shows that there is a *prima facie* case for saying that British policy is in breach of international law at several points. Such breaches make it at least dubious whether Britain can be said to be defending the principle of the rule of law between nations. The silence of the 1998 *Strategic Defence Review*, and of the NATO commissioned Report *Nato in the Twenty-first Century*, on the legal issues of deterrence suggest that not much account is taken of the law in their political and military deliberations.

Post-Cold War Deterrence

So far I have discussed the ethics of nuclear deterrence in largely familiar Cold War terms. This is because recent discussions by principled possessionists show that the fundamental ethical dilemmas have not changed very much. For example, it is still the threat of a re-emergent nuclear-armed Russia which is the 'reference-point' of principled deterrence thinking. It insists that we should not be calculating our deterrence requirements by hopes of deterring Third World dictators with nuclear weapons. This is a very important concession, since much post-Cold War American thinking and, it seems, policy-making by unprincipled possessionists concerns scenarios for deterring Saddam et al., as well as terrorist groups, by threats of nuclear use, not to mention working towards the attainment of 'full spectrum dominance'.[58] Nevertheless it is important to raise the question whether, in the post-Cold War environment, a deterrence scenario could be devised within the boundaries set by morality (and indeed by international law), leading to a new and different basis for the retention of nuclear deterrence. This question must lie at the heart of any adequate appraisal of the British *Strategic Defence Review* (SDR).

Sir Hugh Beach has recently considered a possible scenario for nuclear use in Europe according to the SDR's reasoning.[59] Suppose that a NATO ally – e.g. Hungary – is threatened. Since Britain (along with other NATO states) has given an assurance to all non-nuclear states, other than those already allied to a nuclear state, that it would never use nuclear weapons against them, the only possible use of nuclear weapons in this case would be against a nuclear weapon state, say Russia, or against (say) Ukraine if it were being supported by Russia. Thus the postulate is that Hungary is under a massive conventional threat which can only be countered by a threat of nuclear use from Britain. (The USA and France are presumed not to be involved.) This British threat is supposed to force the aggressor to back off. But what should be the target of this British attack? The Ukrainian forces attacking in Hungary? – but this would devastate much of Hungary itself. Or some appropriate target in Russia? Either way, there is always the possibility that deterrence at this level would fail: the aggressor might not back off, and the 'final sanction' would loom. The likelihood then would be that Russia would retaliate with a nuclear strike against a British city. But would Britain see Birmingham sacrificed for the sake of Budapest?

This is an old Cold War nightmare replayed in a post-Cold War scenario. Is it plausible? – especially given the post-Cold War reality that NATO is greatly superior in conventional forces to any Russian and/or Ukrainian conventional forces which would be engaged in the aggression. The conclusion seems plain: 'the existing doctrine of flexible response should logically be replaced in NATO by a policy under which the use of nuclear weapons by any member of the alliance would be countenanced only in retaliation for use of nuclear weapons against a member of the alliance' (i.e. a 'no first use' policy). This would have the enormous advantage of preparing the way for negotiations for a global Nuclear Weapons Convention, by inviting Russia to revert to its old 'no first use' policy (China is already committed). US weapons deployed in Europe could then be sent back home, and a central European Nuclear Weapons-Free Zone be created. As Sir Hugh Beach concludes, *'There is no reason whatsoever why Britain should not give the lead.'*

Conclusion

One thing that is certainly new, as I said at the beginning, is that there is now a significant body of military, scientific and political opinion which holds that it would be safest for everybody to abolish nuclear weapons as soon as possible. There is today a window of opportunity for doing this, even despite the emergence of India and Pakistan as (effectively) nuclear-weapons states. But it will not stay open for long. While there is still time, the argument goes, humanity should take the plunge, and vote to abolish nuclear weapons by universal treaty. In post-Cold War UNGA meetings a huge majority of the UN member states have regularly demanded such a move, as the votes on the 'Malaysia' resolution of 1997 and 1998 show. Of course nuclear weapons cannot be disinvented, and we all have to face the fact that the knowledge of how to make them will remain with us for the rest of history. But this is not necessarily an objection to negotiating a treaty of abolition, given that Britain supports treaties to abolish other non-uninventable weapons such as biological and chemical weapons and anti-personnel landmines. HMG is already committed to working hard to get to the point where the British deterrent could be included in the negotiating context. Principled possessionism does not disagree with this view as a long-term aim. The nub of the issue is timing: abolition would be a good thing – but not yet. As a corollary, prolonging the present form of non-proliferation regime for the foreseeable future without drastic further steps is thought to be both practicable and desirable. Meanwhile, there are things that could be done in the near future to produce a more stable world, in which nuclear weapons have far less salience than hitherto. Would it not be best, principled possessionism implies, to get on with these measures instead of aiming too high and going too fast, with the probable result of a failure leading to something worse than the admittedly very imperfect situation we now have?[60]

But all of this rests on the nuclear states abjuring any consent, let alone conditional intention, to kill innocents, both as a matter of policy and in their military planning, as well as abiding strictly by international and humanitarian law as demanded by the ICJ. But is this possible? (Whether they would do so even if it were possible is of course a crucial further question.) As we have seen there are extremely powerful reasons for thinking that such a project is impossible, and that even if it were possible we could never be told about it. Past experience of deterrence during the Cold War era reinforces this view, since apparently only a minority of nuclear states have ever thought it worthwhile to attempt such a plan.[61] Of course they have talked a great deal about avoiding such horrors as 'city-swapping'[62] but despite much ambiguous reassurance such talk has mostly not been governed by the *absolute* illicitness of being prepared and willing to kill the innocent in order to achieve the objective. Why should it be, since most of those involved at the 'coalface' do not believe that such killing would be absolutely forbidden? On the other hand contemporary 'abolitionists' hold that the actions of India and Pakistan in testing nuclear weapons signal the dangers of delay. And they are supported by all those who hold that an unequivocal commitment by the nuclear powers to abolition is a *sine qua non* of maintaining the current non-proliferation regime.

In this survey of nuclear pacifism today one cannot better the words of the Holy See to the United Nations on 19 October 1998:

The testing of nuclear weapons by states which stand outside the NPT exacerbates the dangers caused by a weak nonproliferation regime. Nuclear testing by any nation is to be deplored. Criticism of those who test, however, does not deal adequately with the central problem. This is the determination of the nuclear weapons states to carry their nuclear weapons into the twenty-first century, despite their obligation under the NPT to negotiate nuclear disarmament . . . nothing so reveals the negative trend lines in disarmament as the continued insistence that nuclear weapons are essential to national security. The exaggerated claim that nuclear weapons are an aid to peace can only provoke other states to do the same. At this point I would like to recall the Advisory Opinion of the International Court of Justice, that states have an obligation to conclude negotiations leading to nuclear disarmament in all its aspects under strict and effective international control. Moreover . . . the modernization programmes of those who already have nuclear weapons, combined with the acquiring of nuclear weapons by other states, and research now going on in still others, plunge the world into more danger than existed during the Cold War. The longer this situation continues, the more a growing number of states will falsely claim that nuclear weapons are legitimate . . . the world must move more and more towards the abolition of nuclear weapons through a universal, non-discriminatory ban with intensive inspection by a universal authority. This process would begin by the nuclear weapons states committing themselves unequivocally to eliminate their nuclear weapons and without delay to pursue in good faith and bring to a conclusion negotiations to this end. Practical steps to move this process forward should be taken immediately, such as de-alerting and de-activating nuclear weapons. A pledge not to be the first to use nuclear weapons should be made, as an interim step, by every state possessing nuclear weapons. Furthermore it would be a constructive step to hold an international conference on nuclear disarmament in which both governments and civil society could unite their strengths to develop the political will to take the courageous steps necessary for abolition.

Notes

1 Prologue: 'Not as the world gives . . .'

1. The REB fails to reproduce the sense of the Hebrew word *shalom*.
2. Some English versions use the idiom 'well', but the Hebrew has *shalom*.
3. In reverse order, the last being commented on first etc.
4. The REB fails to reproduce the sense of the Hebrew word *shalom*.
5. The familiar Authorized Version rendering, 'Good will towards men', rests on an inferior Greek text and is almost certainly incorrect.
6. R. Eliezer ben Hyrcanus (*c*.100 CE). The prophecy is preserved in the Mishnah (*Sotah* 9.15).
7. This is obscured in the REB, which translates the Greek for 'give' as 'bring'.

2 New Dilemmas

1. The rabbis believed that a 'white lie' may occasionally be permissible where the intention is to promote peace (Babylonian Talmud *Yevamot* 65b).
2. See Harfiyah Abdel Haleem, Oliver Ramsbotham, Saba Risaluddin and Brian Wicker (eds), *The Crescent and the Cross: Muslim and Christian Approaches to War and Peace*, Macmillan 1998, ch.3.
3. This is argued at length in the Appendix.
4. *A History of Europe*, London 1936, p.1172.
5. Sir Brian Urquhart, quoted by Sydney D. Bailey and Sam Daws, *The United Nations*, 3rd edn Macmillan 1995, p.61.
6. See J. and N. Forest, *Four Days in February*, Marshall Pickering 1988.

3 *The Ambiguity of Scripture*

1. See A.E. Harvey, *Retaliation*, The Council on Christian Approaches to Defence and Disarmament 1992, ch.2.
2. See John Barton, *Ethics and the Old Testament*, SCM Press 1998, pp.61ff.
3. Josephus, *Antiquities* 4.296–9.
4. S. Nidditch, *War in the Hebrew Bible*, OUP 1993, identifies several distinct ideologies of war in the Old Testament but has to concede that there is little explicit mitigation of the dominant ethos.
5. A notable exposition along these lines is that of W. Wink, *Engaging the Powers*, Fortress Press 1992, pp.175–93.
6. In 26 CE the Jews successfully put up 'non-violent' resistance to Pilate's threat to introduce images of the Emperor into Jerusalem. In the climate created by this, and by a similar demonstration (again at the risk of their lives) in 39 CE against a still more insensitive threat by Caligula, the saying of Jesus about 'not resisting evil' may have had particular resonance. But this may not have been the original force of the saying. For a balanced discussion, see G. Theissen, *Social Reality and the Early Christians*, T&T Clark 1993, pp.115–56.
7. Already interpreted in Luke 9.23 as a daily discipline. For a list of possible interpretations see J. Schneider in G. Kittel and G. Friedrich (eds), *A Theological Dictionary of the New Testament*, Wm. B.Eerdmans 1964–76, Vol.7, pp.578–79.
8. Sulpicius Severus, *Vita Martini* 3.5.
9. See J. Helgeland, R.J. Daly and J.P. Burns, *Christians and the Military*, SCM Press 1985, pp.22–25, 50–55.

4 *The Just War Tradition Today*

1. Augustine, *Contra Faustum* 22.74. Translation as in John Langan, 'The Elements of St Augustine's Just War Theory' in William S. Babcock (ed), *The Ethics of St Augustine*, Scholars Press, Atlanta 1991, p.171.
2. For Aquinas' views on infidels see *Summa Theologiae* IIa IIae Q.10.
3. See N.Tanner (ed), *Decrees of the Ecumenical Councils*, Sheed and Ward and Georgetown University Press 1990, Vol.1, p.203: 'We prohibit under anathema that murderous art of crossbowmen and archers, which is hateful to God, to be employed against Christians and Catholics from now on' (Canon 29). The

cross-bow was not just a very nasty weapon; it was objectionable also because it was a favourite of low-born soldiers, whose skill with it against mercenaries and brigands threatened the privileged status of the knightly class. On the historical context of this decree see James Turner Johnson, *The Quest for Peace*, Princeton University Press 1987, p.78.

4. Timothy MacDermott, *Summa Theologiae: A Concise Translation*, Eyre and Spottiswoode 1989, p.328.

5. Cf. James Turner Johnson, *Ideology, Reason and the Limitation of War*, Princeton University Press 1975, chs III and IV *passim*.

6. For the view that this problem has caused a breakdown of the tradition of moral philosophy in our own day, see G.E.M. Anscombe, 'Modern Moral Philosophy' in *Collected Philosophical Papers*, Vol. III, Blackwell 1981, pp.26–42.

7. Advisory Opinion on *Legality of the Threat or Use of Nuclear Weapons*, International Court of Justice, The Hague, 8 July 1996.

8. While the Court says that the threat or use of nuclear weapons 'would generally be contrary to the rules of international law applicable in armed conflict', it cannot give a clear ruling on the legality of the threat or use of nuclear weapons 'in an extreme circumstance of self-defence, in which the very survival of a state would be at stake' (Advisory Opinion 105E). This loophole is reminiscent of Michael Walzer's argument about 'supreme emergency' in ch.16 of *Just and Unjust Wars*, Allen Lane 1978. On the other hand, the Court insists (following Article VI of the Nuclear Non-Proliferation Treaty) that 'there exists an obligation to pursue in good faith and bring to a conclusion negotiations leading to nuclear disarmament in all its aspects under strict and effective international control'. This obligation is stressed by the Court without making any reference to 'general and complete disarmament' which is also mentioned in Article VI. The Court appears to regard the obligation to negotiate on nuclear disarmament as a quite separate matter from negotiations on 'general and complete disarmament' despite the fact that some states, in their arguments before the Court, sought to establish an inextricable connection between the two (see John Burroughs, *The (Il)legality of Threat or Use of Nuclear Weapons*, Munster 1997, pp.50 and 122–23).

9. 'All the clerical holy orders are services of the altar on which Christ's sufferings are made present in sacrament. So their office is not to kill or shed others' blood, but rather to be ready to shed

their own for Christ, imitating in very deed what they sacramentally re-enact' (Aquinas, *Summa Theologiae* IIa IIae Q.40 Art.2, trs Timothy MacDermott, p.367).

10. The following two paragraphs, and much of the argument which follows, are taken from a paper submitted by Brian Wicker.

11. See Brian Wicker, 'A Just Defence of Just Prices' in *New Blackfriars*, Vol.77, No.904, May 1996, pp.232ff. for examples. If war is conducted on Clausewitzian 'absolute' principles, notions of proportionality go out of the window. J.F.C. Fuller put this point concisely: 'Clausewitz's insistence that war is a political instrument is the first principle of all military statecraft, but his equal insistence on the complete overthrow of the enemy vitiates the end of grand strategy, which is that a profitable peace demands not the annihilation of one's opponent, but the elimination or modification of the causes of war' (see J.F.C. Fuller, *The Conduct of War 1789–1961: A Study of the Impact of the French, Industrial and Russian Revolutions on War and its Conduct*, Methuen 1961, p.310).

12. Michael Walzer, *Just and Unjust Wars*, ch.10.

13. Theodore J. Koontz, 'Non-Combatant Immunity in Michael Walzer's "Just and Unjust Wars"' in *Ethics and International Affairs*, Vol.11(1997), pp.55–82.

14. Michael Walzer in *Ethics and International Affairs*, Vol.11(1997), pp.102–3.

15. There is also the point made by Elizabeth Anscombe that neglect of the distinction between the innocent and the combatant leads to serious moral damage: 'Pacifism teaches people to make no distinction between the shedding of innocent blood and the shedding of any human blood. And in this way pacifism has corrupted enormous numbers of people who will not act according to its tenets. They become convinced that a number of things are wicked which are not; hence seeing no way of avoiding wickedness, they set no limits to it' (G.E.M Anscombe, 'War and Murder' in *Collected Philosophical Papers*, Vol. III, Blackwell 1981, pp.51–62; originally published in Walter Stein (ed), *Nuclear Weapons and Christian Conscience*, Merlin Press 1961, pp.45–62).

16. For a statement of this argument see Haleem, Ramsbotham, Risaluddin and Wicker (eds), *The Crescent and the Cross*, pp.164–71.

17. When Aquinas insists that war can be just only if waged with a *recta intentio* he has in mind not so much the subjective reflections of the ruler as the aim or purpose of the war he is engaged in.

18. See Roger Williamson (ed), *Some Corner of a Foreign Field*, Macmillan 1998, pp.58–61.

19. When the balance tipped in favour of NATO intervening in Serbia and Kosovo in 1999, allegedly (and unsuccessfully) to prevent further atrocities, many of these questions remained unanswered and returned to call into question the justice of the campaign.

5 Non-Violence and the Pacifist Alternative

1. *The Challenge of Peace: God's Promise and Our Response: A Pastoral Letter on War and Peace*, US Catholic Conference, Washington DC §224.

2. *Peace with Justice: The Official Documentation of the European Ecumenical Assembly*, Conference of European Churches, Geneva 1989, p.60; see also pp.31,42,46,50,95,97, 127,129.

3. *Now is the Time: The Final Document and Other Texts from the World Convocation on JPIC*, WCC, Geneva 1990, p.28.

4. *Programme to Overcome Violence, An Introduction*, WCC, Geneva 1995, p.35.

5. Matt. 5.21–22.

6. Gene Sharp, *The Politics of Nonviolent Action*, Boston, MA 1973. Part 3 lists 198 techniques of nonviolent action.

7. *Centesimus Annus* (1993), 23.

8. As reported by Gene Sharp in 'Beyond Just War and Pacifism', *Ecumenical Review*, Vol.48, No.2, April 1996, p.239.

9. 'Violence, Non-violence and Civil Conflict: The Report of the Corrymeela Consultation' in *Violence, Non-violence and Civil Conflict*, WCC, Geneva 1983, pp.9–15.

10. Sharp, 'Beyond Just War and Pacifism', p.245.

11. *The Nuclear Dilemma: A Christian Search for Understanding. A Report of the Committee of Inquiry on the Nuclear Issue*, Forward Movement Publications, Cincinnati 1987, p.109.

12. For example, John Jorgen Holst, *Civilian Based Defense in a New Era*; Adam Roberts, *Civil Resistance in the East European and Soviet Revolutions*; Olgerts Eglitis, *Nonviolent Action in the Liberation of Latvia*; Roland Bleiker, *Nonviolent Struggle and the Revolution in East Germany*, Albert Einstein Institution, Cambridge MA, Monographs 2, 4, 5 and 6, 1990–93.

13. Pius XI, *Letter to Mexican Bishops*, March 1937: '. . . no reason to condemn citizens for uniting to defend the nation and them-

selves ... against those who make use of the state to drag the nation to ruin'.

14. Christmas Radio Message, 23 December 1956: 'We are in perfect harmony with our predecessors ...'

15. John Paul II, Homily in Coventry Cathedral, 30 May 1982.

16. Roger Wilson, 'Authority, Leadership and Concern' (Swarthmore Lecture 1949) in *Quaker Faith and Practice*, section 24, Quaker Home Service 1995.

17. Quoted in *Advices and Queries*, The Yearly Meeting of the Religious Society of Friends (Quakers) in Britain 1995, §31.

18. John Keegan, *The Reith Lectures 1998: War and our World*, Hutchinson 1998, p.1. This was written before the Nato attack on Serbia in 1999.

19. See Haleem, Ramsbotham, Risaluddin and Wicker (eds), *The Crescent and the Cross*, pp. 207ff., for a reasoned statement of the opposite view.

20. Paul Ramsey's phrase. For a treatment along these lines of Jesus' teaching on poverty see A.E. Harvey, *Strenuous Commands: The Ethic of Jesus*, SCM Press 1990, ch.6.

Appendix: Nuclear Pacifism in the Post-Cold War World

This Appendix was prepared before I had the chance to consult two recent, and valuable, IISS Adelphi Papers: No. 326, by David Yost on 'The US and Nuclear Deterrence in Europe', and No. 327, by Bruno Tertrais, on 'Nuclear Policies in Europe'. Both deal with nuclear deterrence in the post-Cold War era, and come to conclusions very different from those advanced here. However, while Dr Tertrais discusses in some detail certain of the legal points I raise, neither discusses the ethical issue which is key to my argument.

1. Walter Stein (ed), *Peace on Earth: The Way Ahead*, Sheed and Ward 1966, p.7.

2. President Eisenhower, January 1958, quoted in Stein, p.8.

3. R. McNamara, 'Defence Arrangements of the North Atlantic Community', quoted in Finnis, Boyle and Grisez, *Nuclear Deterrence: Morality and Realism*, OUP 1987, ch.1, p.14. The whole of this chapter is worth studying for the examination of the threats made in nuclear deterrence. See also Lawrence Freedman, *The Evolution of Nuclear Strategy*, Macmillan 1981, *passim*.

4. R. McNamara, 'Statement on 1966–70 Defense Program and FY 1966 Defense Budget' (1965) quoted in Finnis, Boyle and Grisez, p.16.

5. *Gaudium et Spes* (1965), 80.
6. I am concentrating here on those ethical objections to the retention of nuclear weapons which are central to the debate about pacifism. There are of course many other objections, commonly made by an increasing number of non-pacifist thinkers, many of which are likely to have more influence on decision-making than a purely pacifist case.
7. A principled possessionist is one who is unequivocally and unconditionally committed both in theory and practice to the two principles mentioned in the section on 'Nuclear Pacifism' below. Sir Michael Quinlan is its best known representative. I have used some of his published work as follows: 'Thinking About Nuclear Weapons', a 'Whitehall Paper' for the Royal United Services Institute (London, RUSI 1997) henceforth cited as Quinlan 1997(1); a talk to RUSI under the same title, cited as Quinlan 1997(2); a commentary on 'The Challenge of Peace' (the 1983 Pastoral Letter by the US Catholic Bishops' Conference) published in *Theological Studies* (Georgetown University), Vol. 48, No.1, March 1987, cited as Quinlan 1987; a paper on 'The Future of Nuclear Weapons' published in *International Affairs*, Vol. 69, No. 3, July 1993, cited as Quinlan 1993; 'The Meaning of Deterrence' in *The Cross and the Bomb: Ethics and the Nuclear Debate*, Mowbray 1983, pp.137–54, cited as Quinlan 1983; 'Nuclear weapons and the abolition of war' in *International Affairs*, Vol. 67,2 (1991), pp.293–301, cited as Quinlan 1991.
8. International groups involved include: the Canberra Commission whose Report on 'The Elimination of Nuclear Weapons' was published in August 1996 by the Australian Department of Foreign Affairs; the Pugwash Conferences, which published 'A Nuclear-Weapon-Free World: Desirable? Feasible?' in 1993 (Westview Press, Boulder, Colorado); Abolition 2000, a coalition of several hundred NGOs designed 'to achieve by the year 2000 an agreement committing the world to the permanent elimination of nuclear weapons according to a fixed timetable'; the New Agenda Coalition, a group of member states of the UN which sponsored a resolution at the UN in 1998 which 'calls for the conclusion, as a first step, of a universal and legally binding multilateral agreement committing all States to the objective of the total elimination of nuclear weapons'; the UN member states which support the so-called Malaysia Resolution, a measure to promote negotiations for nuclear disarmament which has been repeatedly supported by a majority of the UN members at recent

United Nations General Assemblies. The Holy See has taken up the issue of the elimination of nuclear weapons as a priority in its addresses to the UN since 1993.

9. See Canberra Commission Report, p.22: 'the proposition that large numbers of nuclear weapons can be retained in perpetuity and never used – accidentally or by decision – defies credibility'.

10. General Lee Butler, former Commander of the US Strategic Command, and as such responsible for turning deterrence policies into workable military plans, has recently admitted that Cold War deterrence always displayed an 'ultimate inconsistency'. It was 'a circle that could never be squared'. See his contribution to Jonathan Schell's *The Gift of Time*, Granta Books 1998, p.190.

11. 'In contrast to the situation in Europe, it is difficult to see deterrence operating securely against proliferators.' From a speech by Malcolm Rifkind, when Minister of Defence, at the Centre for Defence Studies, King's College London, 16 November 1993, §26.

12. On the UN 'New Agenda' and 'Malaysian' resolutions, sponsored by a variety of states, see note 8 above. It is noteworthy that all the nuclear weapon-possessing states except China voted against the 'New Agenda' resolution. But it is even more noteworthy that Germany under its new centre-left government abstained. This may signify the first 'crack' in the wall of opposition by NATO states against any early start of negotiations.

13. Cf.Archbishop Renato Martino, the Holy See's Observer to the UN, in a speech to the UN on 29 October 1997: 'No weapon so threatens the longed-for peace of the twenty-first century as the nuclear. Let not the immensity of this task (i.e. the elimination of nuclear weapons) dissuade us from the efforts needed to free humanity from such a scourge.'

14. *Gaudium et Spes* (1965), 80

15. The International Court of Justice, in its 1996 Advisory Opinion on the 'Legality of the Threat or Use of Nuclear Weapons' says (§78) that among 'the cardinal principles contained in the texts constituting the fabric of humanitarian law' is the following: 'States must never make civilians the object of attack and must consequently never use weapons that are incapable of distinguishing between civilian and military targets.'

16. That NATO exists to defend, among other things, values which include that of 'the rule of law' is made clear in the 1998 report of the North Atlantic Assembly, entitled 'NATO in the Twenty-First Century', compiled for the fiftieth anniversary of NATO in 1999, p.5.

17. 'The fact is, surely, that we cannot abolish nuclear weapons while maintaining the option, the possibility of major war; what we have to do is to exploit nuclear weapons so as to abolish such war.' We seek 'a structure in which the irreversible fact of nuclear weapons is the keystone of an arch of freedom from war' (Quinlan 1991, p.297).

18. The UK Secretary of State, George Robertson MP, himself seems guilty of this mistake, when he says in his introduction to the British government's 1998 'Strategic Defence Review' (p.2, §7) that 'If we ask our forces to fight, we must be sure they will win.'

19. UN Charter, Article 51.

20. This point was made by Archbishop R. Martino to the UN First Committee, 25 October 1993.

21. Principled possessionists acknowledge that the rationale for nuclear weapons in the foreseeable future must remain to deter a re-emergent Russia; for it is neither wise nor workable 'to try to calibrate our provision by scenarios of third world madmen' (Quinlan 1997(2), p.3). Unprincipled possessionists seem to think differently, however. An American spokesman on the BBC's television programme *The Science of War* on 17 December 1998 spoke of possible uses of 'modernized' nuclear weapons in war-fighting scenarios such as blocking troop movements through mountain passes. Another spokesman on the same programme spoke of a possible requirement, because of technological break-throughs, to modify arms control treaties in order to achieve 'full spectrum dominance' in all possible war-fighting theatres, including outer space.

22. Speech to United Nations General Assembly, 24 May 1978. This passage of Paul VI's speech was quoted and endorsed by John Paul II in his speech to the second special session of the United Nations on disarmament, on 11 June 1982.

23. Butler quoted in Schell, *The Gift of Time*, pp.188–89.

24. This distinction is made by Barrie Paskins, 'Deep Cuts Are Morally Imperative' in Geoffrey Goodwin (ed), *Ethics and Nuclear Deterrence*, Croom Helm 1982, p.103. John Paul II emphasized deterrence 'based on balance' as the only kind that could still be morally acceptable in his 1982 UN speech.

25. Quinlan 1993, p.496.

26. Thus Quinlan 'takes for granted that nuclear attack whose specific purpose was essentially the destruction of population and property, with little regard for combatant/non-combatant distinctions, could never be justified, even in reprisal' (Quinlan 1987, p.17).

Or, to put it more bluntly, he writes in 1997(1), p.3, of 'an essentially city-bashing concept which I would regard as immoral even to plan'.

27. Cf. Lawrence Freedman, *The Evolution of Nuclear Strategy*, Macmillan 1981, p.399: 'An international order that rests upon a stability created by nuclear weapons will be the most terrible legacy with which each succeeding generation will endow the next. To believe that this can go on indefinitely without major disaster requires an optimism unjustified by any historical or political perspective.'

28. My evidence for this paragraph comes from the BBC television programme on *The Science of War*, broadcast on 17 December 1998.

29. Quinlan 1997(1), p.83

30. Quinlan 1997(1), pp.30–31.

31. Evidence given to the US Bishops by public officials in preparation for *The Challenge of Peace* led them to the conclusion that 'the danger of escalation is so great that it would be morally unjustifiable to initiate nuclear war in any form' (144 and 152). Quinlan commented after the publication of this letter that the bishops' estimate was 'neither firmly based nor even plausible . . . It cannot be rated an absolute difficulty; it has to be weighed against the difficulties inherent in other positions' (Quinlan 1987, §22).

32. In trying to mount a pro-deterrence case alongside this incontrovertible prohibition principled possessionists distinguish themselves from those contemporaries – perhaps a majority in most nuclear-weapon states – who do not regard the intentional killing of innocents as absolutely forbidden in all circumstances. For example, see Arthur Hockaday, 'In Defence of Deterrence' in Geoffrey Goodwin (ed), *Ethics and Nuclear Deterrence*, p.84; David Fisher, *Morality and the Bomb*, Croom Helm 1985, ch.3, p.45. For further discussion see Finnis, Boyle and Grisez, *Nuclear Deterrence: Morality and Realism*, pp.181–89.

33. This is a significant point to emphasize. Thus Fisher argues that what matters, in the moral calculus of killing the innocent, is not intention but rather consent. He argues that in the parallel case of abortion the surgeon may well not *intend* to kill the foetus in a hysterectomy operation, but has nevertheless *consented* to its being killed. He could avoid this consequence by refusing consent to the operation (Fisher, *Morality and the Bomb*, pp.33ff.).

34. Cf. Finnis, Boyle and Grisez, *Nuclear Deterrence: Morality and Realism*, p.92.

35. They present them only because they were confronted by a 'former high defence official' who had reflected on their moral analysis of the deterrent problem and replied by making the claim about the avoidance of city-bashing quoted in my text.

36. 'Pure counterforce' here means a use of nuclear weapons to deter in which (a) only the forces used in the enemy's aggression would be threatened, and (b) that all other expected deaths would be truly side-effects, on which the effectiveness of the deterrent threat in no way depended. See Finnis, Boyle and Grisez, *Nuclear Deterrence: Morality and Realism*, ch. VI.5, *passim*.

37. Of course, the foreseen deaths from irradiation of the target area cannot be so dismissed.

38. Quinlan 1983, p.152.

39. Quinlan 1987, §4, p.17.

40. As the 1998 'Strategic Defence Review' makes clear, until quite recently Britain deployed the 'Chevaline' system, which was deliberately designed to penetrate the ABM defences round Moscow. Certainly none of those defence officials interviewed by Jonathan Schell, for his book *The Gift of Time*, so much as hint at plans to abjure in the very last resort all attacks against populations.

41. As Quinlan admits (Quinlan 1991, pp.296–97), 'no theoretical boundary, nor even any peacetime agreement, could be relied upon amid the stresses of war'. He also admits that in the earlier stages of deterrence strategy little interest was shown in planning options designed to confine innocent civilian casualties to the minimum; only later did the USA and the UK (though not necessarily Russia, France or China) 'move significantly' in this direction (Quinlan 1997(1), p.84).

42. Quinlan 1987, §8, p. 18.

43. Cf. Gerard Hughes SJ, in *Heythrop Journal*, Vol. XXIX (1988), pp.224–25.

44. For example, Arthur Hockaday and David Fisher. See above, note 32.

45. For more detail on this point see Finnis, Grisez and Boyle, *Nuclear Deterrence: Morality and Realism*, pp.18–23.

46. Upholding the rule of law is one of NATO's founding principles. Yet the question of the legality of nuclear threats, or of nuclear use, was never raised in the meetings which led up to the 'NATO in the Twenty-First Century' report, published in preparation of NATO's fiftieth birthday in April 1999. On the question of nuclear use or threats of use see 'Legality of the Threat or Use of Nuclear Weapons', Advisory Opinion of the International

Court of Justice, The Hague, 8 July 1996, §105(2)E. Henceforth cited as ICJ Opinion.

47. ICJ Opinion, §105(2)E. Note that the Court treats use and threats of use as legally on a par with each other: 'if an envisaged use of weapons would not meet the requirements of humanitarian law, a threat to engage in such use would also be contrary to that law' (ICJ Opinion, §78).

48. ICJ Opinion, §78, my emphasis added. The ICJ could have made its point clearer by saying 'states must never employ weapons the use of which makes distinguishing civilian from military targets impossible'. Judge Rosalyn Higgins, in her dissenting opinion at the ICJ, insisted that it is 'absolutely prohibited to attack civilians, whether by nuclear or other weapons'.

49. John Burroughs, *The (Il)legality of Threat or Use of Nuclear Weapons*, Munster 1997, p.46.

50. *Strategic Defence Review*, 1998, §63.

51. Letter from C.H.J. Davies, of the Ministry of Defence, to Dr E. Waterson, 27 October 1998. But see also M. Rifkind, §25 (see note 11 above): 'there is sometimes speculation that more so-called "usable" nuclear weapons – very low yield devices which could be used to carry out what are euphemistically called "surgical strikes" – would allow nuclear deterrence to be effective in circumstances where existing weapons would be self-deterring. I am thoroughly opposed to this view.'

52. 'The United Kingdom's nuclear deterrence policy remains entirely defensive: we would only ever consider the use of nuclear weapons in extreme circumstances of self-defence, which includes defence of our NATO allies' (Baroness Symons, Parliamentary Under Secretary of State at the Foreign and Commonwealth Office, House of Lords, *Hansard*, 17 December 1997, col. 687).

53. ICJ Opinion, §105(2)E: 'the Court cannot conclude definitively whether the threat or use of nuclear weapons would be lawful or unlawful in an extreme circumstance of self-defence, in which the very survival of *a* state would be at stake' (my emphasis added).

54. R. Ticehurst, 'Trident and Nuclear Law', address at Law Department, University of Edinburgh, 16 March 1998, p.6.

55. 1998 *Strategic Defence Review*, §62.

56. ICJ Opinion, §105(2)F.

57. The UK has twice voted against the so-called 'Malaysia' resolution, introduced at the UN in 1997 and again in 1998. In its 1998 version (A/C.1/53/L.47) the resolution called for 'total elimination of these weapons with a specified framework of time'. In

1998 this resolution was carried by the First Committee of the UN by 87 votes in favour to 40 against with 15 abstentions. The so-called 'New Agenda' resolution, introduced in 1998 (A/C.1/53/L.48) calls upon the nuclear weapons states 'without delay to pursue in good faith and bring to a conclusion negotiations ...' etc. This resolution was also carried by a large majority, but with the UK voting against.

58. See 'Nuclear Futures: Proliferation of Weapons of Mass Destruction and US Nuclear Strategy' by Hans M. Kristensen (British American Security Information Council, March 1998), and 'Essentials of Post-Cold War Deterrence' (US Strategic Command 1995) – a document released to Kristensen under the US Freedom of Information Act. Cf. 'The Morality of Nuclear Deterrence: An Evaluation' by Pax Christi Bishops in the United States: 'The recent Presidential Decision Directive on nuclear weapons policy ... makes this point clear. The Directive indicates that the United States will continue to rely on nuclear weapons as the cornerstone of the nation's strategic defense, that the role of these weapons has been increased to include deterring Third World non-nuclear weapon states and deterring chemical and biological weapons, as well as other undefined vital US interests abroad.'

59. *Bulletin of the Council for Arms Control*, London, No.32, December 1998, p.3.

60. For such proposals see Quinlan 1997(1), pp.68–72.

61. Quinlan 1997(1), p.84.

62. For discussion of this concept see Finnis, Boyle and Grisez, *Nuclear Deterrence: Morality and Realism*, ch. VI.2, p.139.

General Index

Index of Biblical References